SOMETHING
for the
JOURNEY

Published by
The Bible Reading Fellowship
Peter's Way
Sandy Lane West
Oxford OX4 5HG
ISBN 1 84101 025 1

First edition 1998
10 9 8 7 6 5 4 3 2 1 0

Acknowledgments
New Revised Standard Version of the Bible, copyright © 1989 by the Division of Christian Education of
the National Council of the Churches of Christ in the USA.
Revised Standard Version of the Bible, copyright © 1946, 1952, 1971 by the Division of Christian
Education of the National Council of the Churches of Christ in the USA.
Extract from the Methodist Covenant Service © The Trustees for Methodist Church Purposes. Used by
permission of the Methodist Publishing House.
Extracts from *The Alternative Service Book 1980* are copyright © The Central Board of Finance of the
Church of England and are reproduced by permission.
The Open Gate—David Adams (SPCK). Used by permission.
'When I needed a neighbour' by Sydney Carter © 1965 Stainer & Bell Ltd, London, England.
Extract from the song 'Colours of Day' by Sue McClellan, Keith Rycroft and John Paculabo. Copyright
© 1974 Kingsway's Thankyou Music, P.O. Box 75, Eastbourne, East Sussex BN23 6NW, UK. Used by
kind permission of Kingsway's Thankyou Music.
Extracts from the Book of Common Prayer of 1662, the rights in which are invested in the Crown in
perpetuity within the United Kingdom, are reproduced by permission of the Crown's patentee,
Cambridge University Press.

A catalogue record for this book is
available from the British Library

Printed and bound in Great Britain
by Caledonian Book Manufacturing International, Glasgow

SOMETHING
for the
JOURNEY

Margaret
CUNDIFF

For Peter, in thanksgiving for our
thirty-eight years of marriage, and for our
family life together. Also for the people
of St James' Church, Selby, past and
present, with thanksgiving for the joy and
privilege of ministry over the last twenty-
five years.

> *'And so through all the length of days,*
>   *your goodness faileth never,*
> *Good shepherd, may we sing your praise,*
>   *within your house for ever!'*
>   *(Henry Williams Baker, 1821–1877)*

Acknowledgments

My grateful thanks to my very
patient family, for all their loving
support and good humour.

To my neighbours, Fran and Ian,
for so efficiently and cheerfully translating
my typing into a manuscript.

To my editor, Naomi Starkey, whose
idea this book was, and for all her help,
advice and, above all, friendship.

To all those who throughout my life
have provided 'something for the journey'
at just the right time, and in the
right way.

For the joy of God's Word, which is
indeed 'a lamp to my feet, and a light to
my path' every day.

Contents

Introduction

As I look back on my life, right from childhood, many memories are of my mother saying to me, 'Something for the journey' as she popped a hot potato into my pocket as I went to school on a cold morning, or a packet of homemade biscuits and buns when I went out with the Brownies or Guides. When I went off to college it was an envelope squeezed into my hand as I got on the bus, containing some of her hard-earned money, with those words, 'Something for the journey'. Whenever I went off to distant places there would be those similar little envelopes—'something for the journey'—and even when I was grown up and married and we visited her and Dad, there were always some sweets and chocolates as we said cheerio and got in the car—'something for the journey'. Folk still do it for me even now. One elderly lady in my parish always insists on giving me a couple of sweets when I visit her, 'something for the journey', even though it takes me but ten minutes to get home!

But, of course, that 'something for the journey' was more than cakes, biscuits, sweets or cash. It was and is tender loving care, a token of that bond that is between us. The paper that the token was wrapped in, the smell of home, the familiar handwriting on the envelope, were all part of the sustaining power of love.

In God's word, the Bible, there are, I have found, many gifts wrapped up, placed into my hand and heart by God to cheer, sustain and comfort me, to remind me of him. Sometimes the journey is a long and difficult one, other times just a few minutes in familiar territory, but at all times during my life I have been sustained by God's provision of 'something for the journey'.

We are all on a journey—an overdone expression, I know, but true all the same; and God's word does contain so many gems, treasures, sustaining and enabling us as we travel, giving the assurance of his love, reminding us of his concern for us, and also his expectations of us.

So I would like to share some of these with you. After all, God's gifts are for sharing and it is a pleasure to be able to do so!

I hope that as you share what I have received, you in turn will share with others, for we are all given 'something for the journey' if we will accept it.

So here we go, together, and thank you for the pleasure of your company.

Margaret Cundiff

CHAPTER I

In the beginning

GENESIS 2:7

*Then the Lord God formed man from the
dust of the ground and breathed into his nostrils the breath of
life; and the man became a living being.*

The children listened attentively as their 'Young Church' leader explained that we all began life on earth as babies. We were born unable to do anything for ourselves, and Jesus came into the world like one of us, as a baby, totally dependent on others. All of the five and six year olds accepted that without question, except for John, who said fiercely, 'I was never born. I flew down from the sky when I was two!' The leader patiently listened to John's story and then gently said, 'No, John, you were born as a baby, we all were.' John stuck to his guns. 'Well I wasn't. I flew down from the sky. I know.' One of the other leaders held the trump card—or thought he did. 'John, I have been at this church since before you were born, and I remember you being born and you were a baby.' It made no difference to John, though. 'I told you, I flew down, and I was two. I was *never* a baby.' John stuck to his story which (I have a feeling) was due to the fact that he had a baby sister and could not imagine he had ever been anything like her.

In a few years' time I will enjoy reminding John of what he said, but as for now, if he thinks he flew down from the sky—well, I don't think I or anyone else will be able to persuade him otherwise. We may laugh at a small boy and his strange ideas, knowing full well he will soon come to realize and accept the truth, but what about us? We may not think we were born differently from the rest of the human race, but perhaps we like to believe we have 'hidden extras'—advantages over others. We may despair about our handicaps, or envy those we think were born with 'silver spoons in their mouths'. The question, though, that we all think about from time to time is surely, 'Where did we all begin?' We have all heard and maybe trotted out ourselves the stock answers such as, 'We evolved from monkeys', or, 'We came from God', but what does that tell us? The great thinkers, philosophers, scientists, theologians, have tried to answer that question from the beginning of time. Theories wax and wane in popularity but we are often left with a feeling of being no wiser. There is nothing we can really hold on to, no way of satisfying our longing to know for ourselves.

The Bible states with stark simplicity yet deep profundity, 'In the beginning, God...' Everything began with him 'who was, and is and is to come' (Revelation 4:8). That can be our only starting point. We may wriggle and argue, debate and despair, but there is no way round it. I dare not presume to say I understand all the implications of the account of creation, but I believe, accept and rejoice in it. As I look back at my life, and through the lives of generations before me, stretching back and back until I can see no further, I know that the line stops at a point. And this point is where God created all things. I am part of his wonderful act of creation described in that verse from Genesis. We are all part of what is described as 'the nitty-gritty' of life—the ordinary, everyday, taken-for-granted substance. That is where we came from, and we do well to remember that and keep our feet on the ground when we are tempted to think we are above it! Yet at the same time we are different, not because of what we have done but because when God reached down into the earth he had made, and formed man out of it, he breathed his life into us. The breath of God! We are alive because God has given us life, his life. He has set us free to be ourselves, to have freedom of choice and action. We are not models or robots, but living beings, filled with the breath of God. Dual nationality—feet on earth, hearts in heaven—made to live here on earth, to enjoy life, to make our own unique contribution alongside our fellow citizens of earth, but created to be with God for ever as citizens of heaven. We each have a span of life here on earth, this place we are part of now, and we do not know how long that span will be—thank God for that. Just recently a friend who is very ill confided in me, 'The doctors tell me it is just a matter of time', to which I replied, 'Yes, I know, but isn't it just a matter of time for us all—God's time?'

On a bitterly cold January day I stood in the cemetery and read those familiar words of the funeral service taken from Psalm 103: '...as a father is tender towards his children, so is the Lord tender to those that fear him. For he knows of what we are made, he remembers that we are but dust...' As Nancy's coffin was gently lowered into her grave I thought of her as she had been, confined to a wheelchair for the last thirty years, but so alive with love for her Lord and for all she knew and met. Now as her coffin was held firm by the ground beneath, I continued, 'We have entrusted our sister Nancy to God's merciful keeping, and we now commit her body to the ground, earth to earth, ashes to ashes, dust to dust...' But of course that was not the end of the reading, nor of Nancy, for it went on, '...in sure and certain hope of the resurrection to eternal life through our Lord Jesus Christ, who died, was buried, and rose again for us. To him be glory for ever and ever.' Returning to the dust, yes, but with that sure and certain hope of new life, the new life Nancy had already begun. In spite of the bitterly cold winter's day, the sun shone in all its glory in a brilliant blue sky, and those words shone with the brilliance and joy of heaven. All of us, like Nancy, will return to the dust—at least, the part of us that came from and belongs there will. But the real 'us', the God-given life that God breathed into us from the beginning, remains and returns to the giver.

Genesis 2:7 is a constant reminder to me of where I came from. It also reminds me of where I am going and of the one who travels with me, who has given me my life and the promise of new life. From earth to heaven, the beginning and the end, and all gloriously one, day in day out, God who wonderfully provides all we need for our journey home.

> To all life thou givest, to both great and small,
> in all life thou livest, the true life of all.
> We blossom and flourish as leaves on the tree,
> and wither and perish, but naught changeth thee
>
> Great Father of glory, pure Father of light,
> thine angels adore thee, all veiling their sight.
> All laud we would render, O help us to see
> 'tis only the splendour of light hideth thee.

Walter Chalmers Smith, 1824–1908

CHAPTER 2

The response of love

LUKE 1:46–47

And Mary said, 'My soul magnifies the Lord, and my spirit rejoices in God my Saviour.'

During the 1950s and '60s I worked in industry as a personnel officer for a large textiles firm. We proudly claimed that we looked after our workers 'from the cradle to the grave'. Their welfare and that of their families was of vital importance to us. It paid dividends, of course. We were a family concern: succeeding generations worked for the same company, social life was bound up in working life. There was loyalty, respect and understanding which encompassed boardroom to shopfloor. As personnel officer, I was there not just to 'hire and fire' but to be a friend and support, and my door and ears were always open. Each day I 'walked the mill' through every department, and anything could be discussed—nothing was too trivial. What I learned has stood me in good stead through the years, not least the sense of humour which was a unique forte of the Lancashire textile workers. The annual mill holiday known as 'Wakes Week' was the highlight of the year. Planned for, saved for, talked about all year through, the prospect kept many going when they would have flagged. After all, a week in Blackpool or Scarborough, or just the chance of a rest for a week at home, was a prospect of heaven, worth striving for, living for, waiting for.

Two or three months after the holiday week, I would have more anxious calls than usual upon me, more requests 'for a chat'. It might be the foreman of a department, a mother or aunt who came to tell me of young Joan, Sally or Pat who had 'got themselves into the club'—meaning pregnant—and asking me what could be done. So I would see a young, frightened teenager, usually crying while her elders sat stony-faced. Mothers angry, worried about what the neighbours would say, and scared of what the girl's father would do when he found out. Foremen muttering, 'Well if they will play mothers and fathers, what can they expect?' Sometimes the girl's family would support her, in spite of the 'shame and disgrace', as they called it then, of having an unmarried mother in the family. For some it was a hastily arranged and quiet wedding; others would go to a mothers and babies home, and the child would be either given for adoption or later brought back home and settled into the extended family. For some girls it was a case of being packed off to an understanding aunt in the country, and beginning a new life in the next village or area.

Even now, I can see in my mind's eye some of those young girls who had just discovered they were pregnant, and whose lives had suddenly changed entirely. I heard over the years many versions of how they had come to be pregnant, ranging from ignorance to vivid imagination, but never ever anything like that of Mary. Nor would I have believed such a story either. Yet Mary's account rings absolutely true; I have no problem with it at all. The Virgin Birth is one of the more controversial doctrines of the Christian faith, and has been argued over and discussed for two thousand years. Is it to be taken literally, or spiritually? For me it is both, and more—it is a mystery, a God-given mystery, and I accept it. I can but stand in awe and wonder as I read the account of how the birth of Jesus Christ came about, as I look at Mary and Joseph and their acceptance of God's gift to them, at their transparent honesty and dignity, at their love for one another, their trust in each other and in their God. Matthew, in his gospel account, puts it so plainly and clearly: 'This is how the birth of Jesus Christ came about...' (Matthew 1:18) and each time I read it through, I am more and more convinced of its truth. But what was it like for Mary at the time? No doubt she had the same feelings and fears as any of those young mothers-to-be of my experience, but she had a sure trust in God, and not just trust, but joy. As she goes to be with her relative, Elizabeth, who is also pregnant, she finds someone who knows and understands and rejoices with her. We have the lovely picture of the two mothers to be, meeting. The young girl and the old woman. Elizabeth had given up hope of ever being a mother. She and her husband Zechariah, the priest, had hoped for a family but it seemed never to be. As the years went by, their sadness increased, as to be childless was such a tragedy, and they had gone past the point of even the faintest hope when God answered their prayers. No wonder Zechariah found the idea incredible. Yet it was true, and their son John, which means 'Jehovah's gift', would be the last of the great prophets. He would indeed prepare the way for the Lord, the Saviour, the child who would be called Jesus.

But that was in the future. Let us think of the two women, Mary and Elizabeth, meeting, sharing, rejoicing in God's gift to them: the babies they carried within them, both miracles. One to the young unmarried girl, the other to the elderly woman for whom it had seemed an impossibility. As the two women embraced, so the gifts within them leapt for joy too; and Mary, in her song of praise which has come to be known as the *Magnificat*, puts into words her joy, her faith, and her understanding of the God who acts, who reaches down into our human situation, and who had chosen her to be part of his eternal plan.

Mary looked to God and was content. It did not mean she was without any fear or doubt, or that she was blind to the problems that lay ahead, but she knew the truth, she lived the truth, and she gave birth to the one who was 'the way, the truth and the life' for all humanity. As the life of that child unfolded, she would continually know not only joy but anxiety, fear, and sorrow beyond description. The prophecy of Simeon, as he held the child Jesus in his arms and blessed that family, came terribly to pass. As Mary stood watching her son, in the prime of manhood, dying on the cross thirty-three years later, did she remember those words of Simeon—'...and a sword will pierce your own soul too' (Luke 2:35b)—knowing the awful reality as she stood helpless at the foot of the cross, broken with grief? But all this was in the future; for now Mary and Elizabeth were enjoying the prospects of the new life, the babies who would be born to them. Like any other mothers-to-be, they had plenty to talk about, to look forward to.

Every birth is a miracle. I look back on the birth of our son and daughter, remember them coming into the world, being placed into my arms, and recall looking into the faces of those little ones as they began life here on earth. I too sang, 'My soul magnifies the Lord, and my spirit rejoices in God my Saviour.' I know the joy of motherhood, seeing my children grow up, make their own way in the world, become people in their own right. As children grow, we have to know when and how to let them go, and that is difficult. We want to protect them, hold them, but they have to be themselves. They cannot remain for ever as little children but must grow up, become adults. One of my favourite quotations is, 'There are two gifts you can give to your children—roots and wings.' We provide that safe and loving foundation for life, being there, guiding, sharing, teaching, leading. Then we gently let go, confident that they will find their way home, know where to nest when they need to, safe and secure in that love that will both let them go and draw them home. They are never lost to you, whatever happens.

Mary and Elizabeth would discover that too. Their sons would live strange, amazing lives, so different from any others recorded in history. One would prepare the way for the other to change the story of humankind, the course of history. Both of them would suffer violent deaths, because they lit up the darkness, showed up the dirt, the hatred, the sin, and so were seen as a threat, an embarrassment, something to be got rid of. 'Chop his head off'; 'Hang him high.' John and Jesus, and their mothers, would weep, and their hearts would break, but the words of the *Magnificat* would continue to be sung, to be experienced, to be rejoiced in, in spite of the price that would have to be paid—the price that goes on being paid by those who will, like Mary and Elizabeth, put their trust and hope in God, and in his eternal purposes.

Today, even at this very moment, babies are being born,
making their presence felt by crying loudly to announce their
arrival. Looking round with eyes that seem to have
witnessed other places, fixing on this new world with both
innocence and understanding. Flexing their limbs, eager to get on
with exploring life. Birth is such an ordinary, everyday affair,
so many babies being born every day— each one a miracle,
each one the gift of God.

CHAPTER 3

Learning to live

PROVERBS 22:6

Train children in the right way, and when old, they will not stray.

My mother had a 'saying' for every occasion. She seemed to have the ability to sum up every situation. There she would be, up to her armpits in washing, steam everywhere, and with a nod of her head she would issue forth her words of wisdom. Or, from down on her knees scrubbing the floor—for she believed you could only clean properly by getting down to it on hands and knees—the quick 'two-liners' would be aimed in my direction, and often, with a knowing look, she would put into a few words how she was feeling about the world in general and someone or something in particular. Such sayings as, 'He who trusts in his riches will wither', 'The simple believe everything', 'Better is a dinner of herbs where love is than a fatted ox and hatred with it', 'A hoary head is a crown of glory', 'Good sense makes a man slow to anger', 'Even a child makes himself known by his acts', 'A good name is to be chosen rather than great riches', 'Do not despise your mother when she is old'—and maybe one of her favourites—'Do not boast about tomorrow, for you do not know what a day may bring forth.' I can still hear her voice, with that lovely West Country accent, rolling off those sayings with such feeling for they came right from her heart. They were memorable not just because of the words but because of the rhythm of them. They had poetry, music, beauty and good common sense. If I asked her, 'Mum, where's that from?' she would look puzzled and then reply, 'Oh, it's just a saying', which, more often than not, was the end of that particular conversation. But as I got older and asked about her expressions, those 'sayings', she'd think a bit and tell me how her mother used to trot them out, or how she had learned that particular one at Sunday School, or seen it worked in cross-stitch in a frame in an old friend's home.

She was a great one for remembering old songs, too, and she would sit on my bed at night and sing to me. Some of the songs were very sad. I remember one that began, 'O give me a ticket to heaven, for that's where Dad's gone, they say...' She would explain that it was all about a little girl whose mother had died, and then her father, who was a railwayman, had died too, and she had been told he had gone to heaven. So the little girl had gone down to the railway station and asked for a ticket to heaven so she could join her dad. Well, you can imagine I cried and cried, and my mother cried and cried, as we both sang our sad song. Then she would kiss me and tuck me up in my bed and I would lie awake and worry in case my mother and father died, and I was left all alone. Knowing, though, that my grandad worked on 'God's wonderful railway', the Great Western Railway line between Minehead and Taunton, I felt I would be all right. After all, Grandad could get me my ticket, so I had no need to worry!

As I too went to Sunday School and church, and attended a church school, I heard my mother's 'sayings', plus many more in the same style, read aloud from the Bible. I learned them by heart, I wrote them out at school, and they became part of me. I discovered they were from a book in the Old Testament called Proverbs, and were mainly attributed to King Solomon, who was very wise indeed. I knew by heart the story of his offering to cut a baby in half (1 Kings 3:16–28)—a very exciting tale which fascinated me more than any accounts of great building work carried out by the same king. So I became steeped in the wisdom of the Bible and in the stories of the writers. I came to realize that there was far more to the book of Proverbs than 'sayings'. There was real down-to-earth wisdom, some of which went back a great deal further than Solomon, but it was all centred on a relationship with God as expressed in Proverbs 1:7—'The fear of the Lord is the beginning of knowledge.' The fear of the Lord is where it begins, and on that sure foundation it will be expressed in every area of life. The book of Proverbs is so very relevant to our life today, just as it would have been through the generations who have had some or all of it to guide them. It is also a very optimistic book; it has a confident ring, an assurance that if you follow God's way, then whatever happens you will win through. This was confirmed to me by those who, like my mother, leaders, teachers and friends, not only knew the words but knew the reality of God in their lives. The words of wisdom, the wisdom of God, stood them in good stead and have stood me in good stead too—have become part of me and given me great joy. As I, following in my mother's footsteps, repeat those same 'sayings' I can almost hear her chuckle, and I can happily sing, 'Give me a ticket to heaven...' (not in public, I must add) knowing that my ticket to heaven is based on a far firmer foundation than on a grandad who worked for GWR all his life!

Perhaps that proverb 'Train children in the right way, and when old, they will not stray' is one of the greatest of them all, and is seen to be a reality in many families. But what about when it seems to be a terrible contradiction—just not true? What then?

More and more I am meeting good Christian people who have brought up their children in the faith, doing all they could by prayer and example to give their children a solid and loving basis for their lives, and yet the children have 'gone off the rails', flouted all that goodness and love, and rejected everything they have been taught and shown.

I have sat with people as they have poured their hearts out, cried their eyes out, as they have grieved over their children's present lives. Those parents have looked at me through their tears and said, 'Where did we go wrong?' They have blamed themselves, feeling it must have been their fault. Of course, when we analyse any of our relationships, however close, we know that there have been and still are faults. Maybe sometimes we are too strict, or too lax. Perhaps we have spoken when we shouldn't have, or left unsaid what we could have said. There are always the 'if onlys...' but that does not alter the central fact. Those parents, close relatives, friends, have done all they could and the result has been totally opposite to all they hoped and longed for. So is that verse from Proverbs anything more than wishful thinking?

I remember a minister sharing his grief with me many years ago. His son, who showed such interest in the church, who made a commitment to Christ as a teenager, who was such a joy to them, had turned his back on his family, their way of life, everything they stood for. The minister said, 'I don't know how I can get up in the pulpit and preach, when I know what my son is doing, what sort of life he is leading.' I reminded him of that verse in Proverbs, and he looked at me so sadly. 'If only it was so, Margaret, if only...' It was some years later that the minister got in touch with me again and told me what had just happened. His son had finally emigrated, breaking all contact with the family. It seemed so final, now separated by thousands of miles. There seemed no hope of their relationship being healed. Then came a telephone call from Canada, 'Dad, I have something to tell you, but first will you forgive me for all I have done to you?' The father delightedly said, 'Of course. I love you, of course I forgive you, but what is your news?' and the son poured out the story of how he had started going to church with some friends he had made in Canada. At that church he had opened his heart to God's word, the word he had heard so often in his own home back in England. He had come into a wonderful experience of God's forgiveness and love, but knew that the first thing he must do, like the prodigal son, was to go to his parents and ask forgiveness for all the trouble he had caused, and tell them he wanted to make a new start with God and with his family. There was a joyful reunion on the telephone and later both in Canada and England. The son became a minister himself and brought great happiness and fulfilment to his parents, and to those to whom he ministered in Canada. All right: a happy ending, and there are many, far more than maybe we realize, but the question remains, 'What if nothing seems to happen?' The promise in Proverbs holds good, for in God's economy nothing is wasted. We as parents, godparents, family, friends, teachers, leaders, whatever our relationship with a child, have the privilege and responsibility to train them in God's way and his word. Training by word, by example, by every means possible.

Sadly there are so many broken marriages today, children are brought up in very strange relationships under many pressures, but we have opportunities, all of us, to guide those children. It might be through helping out in a Sunday School, nursery, or playgroup. As a babysitter or carer, as well as within the family situation, we have the opportunity to show God's love to them, to tell them 'the stories of Jesus', to sing songs, read Bible stories. So many opportunities, if only we will see and take them. I am constantly amazed when I meet men and women who say, 'I remember you coming to school and telling us ... Do you remember that verse, it's been such a help to me ... I thought of you when I heard ...' So do not lose heart. Go on praying, sowing the seeds, telling, reading, singing, and holding to that promise, 'Train children in the right way, and when old, they will not stray.' Give them something for their journey through life, something to hold on to, something which may lie hidden for many years, but is there for rediscovery when needed. Think of the dying thief beside Jesus, the one who turned his head in his dying moment and said, 'Jesus, remember me when you come into your kingdom' (Luke 23:42). Could a memory have been stirred within him of what he had been taught as a child in the synagogue about the coming Messiah, the Saviour? Perhaps he remembered the teaching of his parents, who instilled in him a sense of right and wrong, even though he had disregarded what he had been taught? A seed sown in his heart many years ago? We will never know until we too join him in heaven, we too enter into the joy of the Lord, when all will be revealed, and, I believe, the truth of that verse from Proverbs gloriously affirmed and rejoiced in. It will be then that earth's yesterdays are caught up in heaven today.

Lord, Sometimes it takes a lot of faith, imagination and hope to really believe those words from Proverbs, faced with so much evidence to the contrary—or so it seems.

I meet despairing parents who have done their best to bring their children up in your way, with love and understanding, and now see it all rejected.

What can I say to them? What can I do?

Maybe all I can say or do is stand with them, and point to your unfailing love and power, which reach beyond what we can see or understand, and the truth of your word which is for all eternity.

And I can encourage them to go on praying, loving and trusting, enabled by your life-giving and life-restoring Spirit.

CHAPTER 4

Open to God

1 SAMUEL 3:10

*Now the Lord came and stood there, calling as before, 'Samuel!
Samuel!' And Samuel said, 'Speak, for your servant is listening.'*

There was something familiar about this radiantly happy mother
standing there with her young son, but the old priest could not
place her, although he was sure he had met her before. Then she
said, 'I am the woman who was standing here in your presence,
praying to the Lord. For this child I prayed; and the Lord has granted me the petition that I made to him.' Of course! Eli remembered
her coming to the temple, it must have been three or four years
ago. She had been in deep distress, crying and wailing, in fact he
thought she was drunk, such was the state she was in, and he had
rebuked her sternly. But she had explained that she was crying her
heart out before God, for she longed desperately for a child, and
her prayers had gone unanswered. Elkanah, her husband, was a
kind and loving man, but his other wife, who had children, tor-
mented her for her childlessness, making her life a misery. Eli had
felt dreadful for misjudging her. She was obviously a good woman
who deserved to have her prayers answered, so he had blessed her
and told her, 'Go in peace: the God of Israel grant the petition you
have made to him.' His words brought her peace and comfort, that
was obvious, for she stopped crying and looked a different woman
as she went away.

Now here she was, Hannah with her son Samuel, the answer to
their prayers. What a wonderful picture they made standing there,
giving thanks. But what was so surprising was that she had not
come just to give thanks for answered prayer but to give the child
back to serve the Lord, to train as a priest under the care of Eli. As
Hannah said of her son, 'I have lent him to the Lord.' She would
come with her husband each year to see him, bring clothes for
him, but from now on he was to be with Eli. Eli must have felt
encouraged through this woman's wholehearted commitment to
God and her faith in him, but also apprehensive. His own two
sons had turned out worthless, evil men, taking advantage of their

position in the temple to defraud those who came to pray. Not only that, they were living immoral lives with the women who were the servants of the temple. So the whole life of the temple was a sham, a disgrace, and the old priest had been unable to do anything about it. His sons merely laughed at him when he urged them to change their ways. He reminded them that they had sinned against God as well as their fellow human beings, and that God would punish them, but it was all to no avail. How could Eli undertake the training of this young boy when he had been such a failure as a father and a priest? Yet he knew it was God's will, so he would care for the boy, train him, protect him.

As the boy grew he brought great joy to Eli, who saw the boy growing strong in body, mind and spirit, eager to learn, eager to serve. But what of the future? The forces of darkness seemed to be closing in, worship was at an all-time low, and in a few terse words the situation is put plainly: 'The word of the Lord was rare in those days, there was no frequent vision' (1 Samuel 3:1). What could an old man, whose sight was almost gone, who had been unable to influence his own sons, let alone the community, give to the boy entrusted to his care? Wouldn't Samuel have had a better training at home with his God-fearing mother than here, surrounded by failure and sin, in an environment that spelt disaster?

Yet one night in the temple, Samuel was to meet with God, personally and dramatically—and the agent of that meeting was Eli, for it was he who recognized that God was calling Samuel. It was he who instructed the boy to open his ears and his heart to God with the words, 'Speak, for your servant is listening.'

That night the relationship between God and Samuel was sealed. In the future Samuel would lead the people as judge and priest and, later on, would anoint Saul and David as kings. He became a great man, because he had learnt as a child to listen to God and to obey his word. As he listened and obeyed, then he could speak with authority, God's authority. He became God's man for that crucial time in history. For Eli, the word of the Lord was terrible. His sons would die, and so would Eli—that would be their punishment, and Samuel had to tell Eli. In fact, Eli insisted on being told. He did not rant or rave, did not complain or argue, but accepted the judgment of God. 'It is the Lord, let him do what seems good to him' (1 Samuel 3:18).

As we look at the holy and great man Samuel, we should see also Samuel the child. On one side of him, his mother Hannah and her offering to God of the greatest gift she had, her firstborn son. Her action must have seemed so strange to those around her, and she probably came in for a great deal of criticism. Some may have thought her mad to do such a thing, and how did her husband feel? After all, Samuel was his son too. Hannah kept her vow, her promise, but it must have been hard for her. She had to trust God and also trust Eli. In view of the situation at the temple, did she not have fears and doubts? She stepped out in faith and obedience, trusting God and man, and her faith and obedience were rewarded through what her son became, the contribution he was enabled to make that influenced the course of history. What about Eli? The one on the other side, who received that child, cared for him, instructed him, protected him? Samuel became for him the son he had longed for, to continue the work as a true priest, a wise judge, to restore the glory of the Lord and to bring peace and justice for all the people. Between them, Hannah and Eli had the making of the man. We can never overestimate the contribution of a mother's love and prayers, and Hannah would continue that loving and praying for her son all her life.

I see that same love and prayer in the lives of so many mothers for their children. They never cease to love and pray, whatever happens, whatever the circumstances. Many have the joy of seeing their children grow up, like Samuel, to be a blessing and a joy, to make an important contribution to the life of society. I go into homes where photographs of smiling, confident graduates have pride of place. I read the press cuttings, and share the delights of proud parents. I go into other homes where I weep with grieving parents whose children have gone off the rails, have seemed to discard all the values their parents tried to instil in them, who have brought disgrace and despair. Yet those parents go on loving and praying, and I encourage them to do so, for I know that love and prayer are answered, even though it may take a long time, and take a strange turn. Love and prayer are never ever wasted, never ever go unheard. 'Don't ever give up,' I plead, although I know it is often very hard for them to continue. I have the joy of seeing our own children living good and useful lives. We have a close and happy relationship, so you could say it is easy for me. Yes, it is, and

I thank God it is as I go on loving and praying each day for them, and thanking God for all he has done in their lives, for all I can enjoy too through them. I also realize that no one is immune from tragedy, suffering, failure, disgrace, and I do not know the pressures they will have to face; so love and prayer are the order of each day for them, handing them over to the Lord. Above all, my prayer is that they, like Samuel, will listen and hear what the Lord will say to them, and have the strength and grace to obey. What I pray for our children I pray for the children God has entrusted to us in the church family and in the village school at the back of our house, the neighbours' children who play games at the front, those happy, smiling, polite children. But then there are the sad-looking, defiant, loud-mouthed youngsters who take a delight in causing trouble, getting into mischief, stealing, cheating, drinking, smoking, drug-taking, seemingly without any sense of the mess they are getting into, because no one bothers, no one loves, no one prays. No one? I hear that gentle but firm voice of God saying, 'No one— what are *you* doing about these my children, Margaret?' I remember last week on the underground train seeing a youngster high on drugs, slashing away at the window and the seats, eyes rolling, movements jerky, and I wanted to reach out and say, 'Don't do that!' but I didn't because, like everyone else, I was scared of him. I have thought of him a lot since then, as I have been thinking again about the boy Samuel and his mother Hannah and the old priest, Eli, recognizing their contribution in making him the man he became. A child in the temple, a boy on a train... but then who has ever loved the boy on the train, who has ever prayed for him? What chance has he got?

> Lord, You are speaking to me words I do not really want to hear.
> You are reminding me of the boy on the train with whom
> I was angry, whom I despised, feared. You were telling me you
> love him, you wanted him to know that, you wanted him to
> experience love and care and I missed the opportunity you gave
> me. Forgive me, remind me of him, that I might hold him
> in love and prayer. That is all I can do, all you ask me to do,
> all I need to do—and I can leave the rest to you.

CHAPTER 5

Get yourself a life

MARK 8:34–37

*He called the crowd with his disciples, and said to them,
'If any want to become my followers, let them deny themselves
and take up their cross and follow me. For those who want
to save their life will lose it, and those who lose their life for my
sake, and for the sake of the gospel, will save it. For what
will it profit them to gain the whole world and forfeit their life?
Indeed, what can they give in return for their life?'*

I was standing at the church door at the end of the morning service, shaking hands with the departing members of the congregation, when Eddie rushed up to me, looking rather anxious. 'Hey, Margaret, you know what you said this morning about that man who was told to sell everything he had and give it all away? Does it mean that if I'm a Christian I've got to sell up, give everything away, be left with nothing? What happens to us then?' I could tell by Eddie's face that he was genuinely worried about the implications for him and for his family if that was the case. 'Well, here Jesus was speaking to one particular individual whose possessions were the stumbling-block between him and following Jesus wholeheartedly. He knew that, and Jesus did too.' Eddie was not going to be put off that easily. 'But he said it, Margaret, you can't get away from that.' I tried another tack. 'What it's all about is whether Jesus is first in our lives, or just part of it. Is there anything that matters more to us than him, anything we would hang on to, come what may? It is a question of what or who has priority in our lives.' Eddie looked thoughtful, 'Hmm, yes, I suppose that is it, but it's something that has always puzzled me really.' I had a feeling as Eddie left church that it would not be the last time he would bring up that particular subject.

As I walked back into the vestry I thought about the young man who came running to Jesus, kneeling down and asking how he could inherit eternal life—what would he have to do to be sure of it? He was a seeker, a good man, a rich man, a thoughtful man. He knew what he really wanted more than anything, and he was prepared to do anything to have it. He also recognized that Jesus held the answer, Jesus *was* the answer, and now here he was with Jesus, when all would be revealed. It was revealed, and so was he, for faced with the answer he was unable to pay the price. What he already had was worth more than what he would receive. He had so much to give. As Jesus looked at him he loved him, wanted to share with him the adventure of living for God, but the young man was not free. He was chained to possessions. He did not own them, they owned him, and he was their slave. Jesus offered him freedom, offered him eternal life, all the young man had to do was let go—and he couldn't. 'You lack one thing; go, sell what you own, and give the money to the poor, and you will have treasure in heaven; then come, follow me.' The gospel says of that young man, 'He was shocked and went away grieving, for he had many possessions' (Mark 10:21–22).

My thoughts turned to Eddie again, remembering how over the years I had seen him grow in his faith, in love and service. Always willing to face up to hard decisions, ready to work out problems honestly and openly. A follower of Jesus, right there with him, discovering as he went the secret of eternal life. Where was it leading him? I wondered. But one thing I was sure about—Eddie would stay with it, whatever it cost. What about that young man, anyway? Did he go away, or did he return, having freed himself of that which hindered his calling? Did he discover, then or later, the joy of eternal life, of following the way of Jesus? Did he save his own skin, or inherit the kingdom of heaven?

The subject turned over and over in my mind during the next few days, and while sorting out some papers I found a small booklet called *My Journey*, by Sylvia Wright. She was challenged by those words, 'Go sell all that you have, give to the poor and follow me...' A Yorkshire nurse, aged forty-two, she did just that, selling her house and some land she had, drawing out her pension contributions and savings and going out to India to set up a clinic, then a hospital; and the work has gone from strength to strength. But this is no fairy story. It has often been difficult and she writes, 'On a personal level my life has been far from easy. I have experienced great loneliness and known much misunderstanding, and have been deeply hurt many times ... I pray always for God's guidance, and have great trust in him. What the future holds I do not know. I try to leave all in God's hands and go where he leads. Nothing is easy.'

The same week I picked up the daily paper and read the story of a British Airways dispatcher who, on holiday in Ghana, discovered a school which was just a tree, the children and their teacher huddled beneath it. 'What happens when it rains?' he asked. 'School stops,' he was told. He says that in that instant he realized he could not return to the comfort of what he had, without helping the children. He returned to England as a man with a mission, to build a school. Now, four years on, there is a new school for the children, called 'The Lord is my Shepherd Educational Centre'. Dave Mustill—that's his name—admits that the school has taken over his life, drained his energy and personal savings, but he has done what he had to do. He does not claim to be religious, but he fits the bill of the words of Jesus, 'By their fruits you will know them.'

In front of me is today's paper with the headline 'Woman sells house to fund church repairs', telling the story of a woman, who wishes to remain anonymous, who has sold her house and given the proceeds to the church. She said in a letter, 'This was always a gift from the Lord. My part in it is purely incidental. It might have been anybody. Let us thank God and look to the future.' Her rector says of her, 'It actually involved considerable sacrifice. But it wasn't a rash act of writing the cheque and regretting it afterwards. The person had her decision confirmed through prayer and reading the Bible over the last twelve months.'

A hospital in India, a school in Ghana, a church in Somerset— what they all have in common are people who sat light to their own possessions and gave, out of love. And it goes on happening, day in, day out, as more people than we could ever imagine find the way of freedom through giving, and in doing so discover for themselves that walking the way of the cross, the way of sacrifice, is the path of life. It may be through giving up money, possessions, time, opportunities, promotion, comfort or even repute. It may be dramatic or gentle and hidden, but it all hinges on that denial of self, and openness to God and their fellow human beings. What does this have to say to us and what we possess? It is a matter of our priorities in life, what matters most to us. At the end of the day—and of life—what does count, what really matters, what is of real value?

It is said that the last words of Queen Elizabeth I were, 'All my possessions for a moment of time.' She had power, wealth, authority. She was a great queen who commanded absolute obedience. Whatever she desired was hers; a word from her, even a glance, could decide the fate or fortune of her citizens. The period of history marking her reign, the Elizabethan age, sparkles like a jewel for all time, but she was human like any other person, like you and me. She was born, she lived and then she died. What counted as she passed from this world to the next? Let us not dwell on speculation, on things known only to God, but heed the words of Jesus, what he asks of us personally, whether we are prepared to let go and go with him or… Only we can make that decision.

Lord, I don't have 'great possessions', not like that
young man who came running to you, and certainly not like
many people I know, but then I have far more than
many others. In fact I have plenty, enough—and more than
enough. Valuable? Well, they are to me. Some I have
had a long time, bought because I liked them, given to me by
friends and relatives. Earned through hard work, by being
'careful'—and what is mine is mine. A bit in the bank, there for
'a rainy day', security for the future—we all need that,
don't we, these days? How important are these things to me?
Not very. Well, not all that important, not 'a matter of
life and death' important. Could I give them up if you asked me
to? Now I will have to think hard about that one, won't I?
But if it is the choice between them and you, between
death or life, then… you win! After all, I want to get my
priorities right. Thank you for reminding me!

CHAPTER 6

Bridging the gap

GENESIS 28:16–17

*Then Jacob woke from his sleep and said, 'Surely the Lord is in
this place—and I did not know it!' And he was afraid,
and said, 'How awesome is this place! This is none other than the
house of God, and this is the gate of heaven.'*

Jacob is not a character I warm to easily, as he possesses many
unpleasant traits. He is jealous, devious, a liar and a cheat. Yet from
this very unpromising start he became a mighty man of God. For
unlikely as was his beginning, God had his hand upon him, and
Jacob was rescued from himself, to truly be himself. Jacob was
dogged by negative circumstances from his birth. Not just because
he was the second-born of twins, but through his personality, his
lifestyle. While his elder brother Esau was very much 'a man's
man'—the tough, strong hunter, the joy of his father Isaac, who
saw in him a worthy and able successor—Jacob was the quiet, stay-
at-home 'mother's boy', resentful of his outgoing, physically strong
and able brother; and his jealousy seems to have been fuelled by
his mother Rebekah. A family situation bound to explode violently and with tragic consequences. A divided family, favouritism
shown by the parents driving a wedge between the brothers. An
old story, yet sadly ever new. While the elder brother was out hunt-
ing, Jacob was at home doing the cooking. If only their parents
could have seen their complementary roles rather than comparing
them with each other! While Jacob learned to cook, he also cooked
up a scheme to cheat his brother out of his birthright, and the day
came when the hungry hunter was easily persuaded to sell his
inheritance to his younger brother for a dish of stew. So what?
What difference would that make to the future? Probably Esau
thought no more about it, but Jacob and his mother planned the
next stage with cunning and care. Time went by, and the plot
thickened. It was all a matter of time.

It was time that caught up with Isaac, elderly, feeble, almost
blind. He knew he was close to death, but with his beloved Esau
at the helm all would be well. Just one special last meal with his

son—fresh meat, the skill of the hunter providing it, and preparing it—and then the blessing, so that he could die in peace. With the hunter safely away chasing the prey, Rebekah saw this as the chance for Jacob to secure the blessing. After all, he knew how to prepare a good meal. The problem was that while Isaac could not see, he could smell, and knew well the smell and feel of his hairy, outdoor son. Rebekah, though, was a step ahead, and by putting animal skins on her son Jacob, and dressing him in Esau's clothes, she enabled him to pass for his brother. So the old man was tricked into giving his blessing to the 'smooth' Jacob while his brother was still out catching the ingredients for his meal.

It does not take much imagination to visualize the scene when Esau, proud and happy with his catch, came back home to his father, to find they had both been cheated. The distraught old man, and the anger—and righteous anger too—of Esau, who was determined to kill his lying, scheming younger brother, frightened Rebekah, and she realized she would lose both her sons. One would kill, the other be killed, and she would lose everything. So, quick-thinking as ever, she sent Jacob away to a place of safety, to her brother Laban in Haran, hoping that the time would come when what had happened might be forgiven and forgotten.

So who was to blame in this sorry tale? Was it the parents, showing such favouritism, the brothers' rivalry, the deviousness, lack of acceptance, the breakdown of relationships between the family members? It was a combination of many things over the years that led to that final break-up, which left all their lives shattered.

As I pick up today's newspaper, turn on the radio or switch on the television, the same story is repeated over and over again. The account from the book of Genesis appears in today's editorial in *The Sun* and *The Times*, on the lunchtime news, in the documentary, and in a few brief lines on teletext. Jealousy, intrigue, deceit, feuds, bitterness, hatred, violence, often culminating in death. Can anything be salvaged or will there be that 'knock-on' effect from generation to generation? Look again at Jacob, on the run, afraid of his brother who even now might catch up with him and despatch him as easily as he would a wild animal. Away from the love and protection of his mother, the security of home, out in the dark and the cold, Jacob had hit rock bottom. His plans had come to nothing, and he was even worse off now, totally isolated. In the dark, with a stone for his pillow, he sleeps the sleep of exhaustion, and right then, at that moment, when he has nothing at all, he makes the biggest discovery of his life. God was there with him, there was hope for the future, a new life to be had. Not by scheming, planning, deceiving, cheating, but a gift given freely by God to him. He in turn would serve God, his God. That foretaste of heaven, with the vision of angels and of the presence of the Lord beside him, blessing him, encouraging him, would remain with him for ever. He did not have to strive to be accepted, he knew he was accepted and blessed as himself, and now he would live his life in that knowledge and strength. The rest of the story is, as they say, 'history'. Jacob did not turn into a paragon of virtue overnight, and he did not find life easy. He was still devious, worked some very strange deals and had some very nasty tricks played on him—not least in affairs of the heart, finding his bride was not the one with whom he had fallen in love, but her older sister. Ironic, really, when you think what he had gained through being substituted for his elder brother by a scheming mother. Now the tables are turned on him when a scheming father substitutes an elder daughter for her younger, beautiful sister. History has a way of repeating itself!

Yet in all this Jacob knew a personal relationship with God, his God. He knew that God was with him, would be with him. And whatever happened, one day the promise, the blessing and the vision would be fulfilled.

In the sordid stories of today, as we look at the seemingly hopeless situations splashed across the front pages, we try to grapple with our own failures and inadequacies, to come to terms with the effect of sinning and being sinned against in our own lives. In the darkness and despair, on the stony ground, can we find help, strength? Dare we hope for a blessing? The answer is yes. Many times in my own life I have experienced the glorious reality of those words of Jacob, 'Surely the Lord is in this place, and I did not know it!' Times when I have felt so alone, afraid, angry with myself, and with others. Times of extreme weakness, when I have made an absolute mess of something I really wanted to do well, when I have failed others I love, have been plunged into despair. It has been in just those situations when I have had my vision of angels, known without doubt the presence of the Lord; and the situation has been transformed so that right there and then I knew I was in a holy place, the gateway to heaven. I have never forgotten, many years ago now, someone saying, 'When you feel at the end of your tether, remember who holds the other end.' At that time I knew it was a word for someone else, and I saw the effect it had on him, lifting him up out of the darkness, the despair, into hope and life. Since then I have known it for myself, as a word for me, a transforming word, a renewing word, enabling me to resume my journey with joy and anticipation. But what about those stories I read and hear and see today through the media coverage? What about sickening, depraved behaviour, violence, abuse, cold, calculating evil as well as unfettered mindless power let loose? It happens in homes, institutions, 'high places', in fact can happen anywhere, anytime. Where is God? Are there places so dark, so disgusting, that he cannot be, cannot touch, cannot heal? Where angels not only fear to tread, but do not venture? Where the voice of love, the balm of blessing, cannot be experienced? Anywhere so completely closed and shuttered that a vision of heaven cannot break it open? I know, deep within myself, in my own experience and through the experiences of others, that there is no place, nowhere, no situation on earth where God is not already present, for this is his world, his domain, and his love is stronger than all the forces of evil, of darkness and death. God does not have 'no go' areas. No place is too dark, no life too barren and stony.

There is a ladder set up from earth to heaven; the gap has been bridged from the deepest depths to the height of glory. Whether we are stuck on the bottom rung, halfway up or near the top, we may see life from a different perspective, but the point is that we are being enabled by God's grace to move from darkness to light. God is for us. He has provided not only an escape route but assistance on our journey, for angels come in all shapes and sizes, and often from quite unexpected quarters. There are many surprises on our way—an answered prayer, a helping hand, a glimmer of light, all make for encouragement even on the darkest day, the hardest climb.

As I reflect on those angels that came to the aid of Jacob, the angels I meet on my journey, and who make life easier for me, I realize that 'angels in all shapes and sizes' might have room in their number for even someone like me, willing to learn, willing to utter a timely prayer, to give a smile of encouragement or 'a lift up' to a modern-day Jacob in a stony and dark place. Perhaps then they might be enabled to lift their head, open their eyes and say, 'Surely the Lord is in this place and I did not know it!' and begin on the long journey home with God.

> *Lord, In the world's dark places, shed light, give hope.*
> *In the hearts of the despairing, shed light, give hope.*
> *In the lives of the caring, shed light, give hope.*
> *In the events of this day, shed light, give hope.*
> *For the future and all that lies before us, shed light, give hope.*

CHAPTER 7

Is anyone out there?

LUKE 10:33–34

But a Samaritan while travelling came near him;
and when he saw him, he was moved with pity. He went to him
and bandaged his wounds, having poured oil and wine
on them. Then he put him on his own animal, brought him to
an inn, and took care of him.

My Auntie Win was what you would call a bit of a character—in fact she was full of it! In the days when it was considered 'not the thing' for young ladies to be adventurous, outspoken and boisterous, my aunt was all of those and much more. Extremely sporty, she excelled in a wide variety of activities, and was always on the look-out for new challenges. She found a new and exciting one in riding a high-powered motorcycle. Sadly she was involved in an accident and had to have a leg amputated. This seemed the end of her hopes and dreams, and at the age of twenty-two she felt as if life was over. While she was in hospital her boyfriend proposed to her. She was quite overwhelmed, and felt that maybe he was just sorry for her, so she insisted on waiting until she could walk down the aisle on her artificial leg—no mean feat, but she felt this would give her boyfriend time to change his mind if it had been a hasty decision. He did not change his mind, neither did she, and they walked together as husband and wife for many, many years until his death. In spite of having an artificial leg and suffering great pain, especially as she got older, she never lost her sense of fun and adventure. She was the life and soul of every party—and how she enjoyed parties—and no challenge was too great for her. After my uncle's death, her stroke, and increasing ill health, she needed to move into special sheltered housing, and was confined to a wheelchair. But this did not hamper her adventurous spirit, and she decided that if she had an electric three-wheeler wheelchair she would have the freedom to get around on her own. This proved to be a very near disaster. Travelling through the gardens near her home in Bridgwater, she accidentally put her foot on to the accelerator instead of the brake. Out of control, the wheelchair roared on towards the river bank, hit a tree and my aunt was catapulted into the River Parrett. Fortunately the river was at low tide, and so she landed in a bed of smelly, sticky mud, a soft but dirty landing. Stuck there, unable to help herself, and absolutely covered in filthy mud she shouted for help. Some people just looked at her, not daring to go and help, others muttered that she should not have been allowed out in that chair, not at her age, and with her disabilities, others shouted for someone to come and help, and yet another ran to a phone to dial 999. Then three young men who were in the park came running, clad in their boots and tight jeans, wearing earrings and sporting brightly coloured 'Mohican' haircuts—the sort of young men who attracted 'tut-tutting' and much shaking of heads, with the comments, 'Lazy young layabouts, up to no good…'. Straight into the river they went, covered in mud, but together they managed to get my aunt to safety, keeping her cheerful with their encouragement, and laughing together at the state they were all in. The ambulance came and took her to hospital, cleaned her up, and she was none the worse for her adventure, but she decided there and then to give up the electric wheelchair. 'Bit too powerful for me at my age,' she confessed.

Her photograph together with the lads who rescued her appeared in the local paper, all of them smiling, with the comments from my aunt, 'Some people complain about the younger generation, but I think they are wonderful. They saved me, lovely lads!' She so enjoyed recounting the tale, and she was always creased with laughter as she described that feeling of shooting through space and landing in the mud. She had nothing but praise for the lads who rescued her, who thought nothing of their own skins or clothing, or what they looked like down there in the mud with her. She said, 'I don't suppose anyone else would have done it, but they knew what it's like to be down on your luck, stuck in the mucky end of life.' And then she'd roar again with laughter remembering her very special day. A very special lady she was too, with a wonderful sense of humour and an understanding and love of people, all sorts of people. She died in her eighties, having lived an extremely fulfilled life, giving pleasure to everyone who met her.

Whenever I read or hear the story Jesus told of the good Samaritan, my thoughts always go to my aunt in the mud and her three good Samaritans—the unlikely lads, those who were viewed with suspicion because of their dress, their lifestyle, but who, when the crunch came, were the ones who came to the rescue. Like the Samaritan in the story, they knew what it was like to be at the bottom end of society, looked down on, ridiculed and dismissed as of no value. The priest and the Levite were such busy people, had important business to attend to as valued members of society. They could not afford to be delayed, put in danger because of one traveller's misfortune. They were sorry for him, of course, but his misfortune just went to prove how careful you have to be when you travel. It all showed how much times had changed, and for the worse. There were times when you could have travelled without a thought for safety, but this poor man now (they might have said), well it all goes to prove, doesn't it?

All goes to prove that decent, good, responsible people—like you and me too, dare I suggest—can view suffering and need in such a dispassionate manner. Have we become so used to seeing it, especially through the media coverage, that it no longer touches us? Or are we so concerned about ourselves, our own survival, our own plans, that we can pass by on the other side? Maybe we are sometimes tempted to pass judgment on the unfortunate victims, feeling, 'Well, they were asking for it.' Thank God for those who, like the Samaritan, see someone in need and respond wholeheartedly, regardless of who they are or what it might cost. Perhaps we need to know what it is like to be an outsider, despised, rejected, as the Samaritans were, or like the young men who rescued my aunt, knowing what being in a mess—literally—was like. Then we can feel the pain of a fellow sufferer, and respond with heart and soul, a spontaneous response to a cry for help.

Time and time again I have found it is the people who could do with help themselves who respond so willingly to help others. I am constantly amazed by the generosity and warm-hearted response that comes from those who are hard pressed to look after themselves, keep their heads above water, get through each day. I think of one lady in particular who always responds with, 'There's plenty worse off than me, Mrs Cundiff, I like to help if I can'—and I know she can't afford to, really, but she does, and does so cheerfully and generously.

I remember when Bob Geldof first took up the cause of the people of Ethiopia. I have to say that he was, in my poor opinion, the last person I would have imagined getting so much involved in the plight of refugees a world away from his lifestyle, because of his (what I thought then) self-opinionated way of living. Yet through his efforts millions must have been saved from starvation, from dying a terrible death. I had only seen a wild pop singer, who needed a shave and a decent haircut; for the refugees he proved to be a saviour. Maybe I have learned a lesson through him that I will do well to remember—and more than remember, to follow.

Why did Jesus tell the story of the good Samaritan? To shake people like the lawyer who asked the question, and like me too, out of complacency, out of making excuses, out of being judgmental, and enable us to see the real issues and values of life. It is not enough to recognize those who are showing love, care, compassion and mercy. We need to respond also to the command of Jesus, 'Go and do likewise,' and to that there is only one answer—action.

> *When I needed a neighbour, were you there, were you there?*
> *When I needed a neighbour, were you there?*
> *And the creed and the colour and the name won't matter,*
> *were you there?*
>
> *I was hungry and thirsty, were you there, were you there?*
> *I was hungry and thirsty, were you there?*
> *And the creed and the colour and the name won't matter,*
> *were you there?*
>
> *When I needed a healer, were you there, were you there?*
> *When I needed a healer, were you there?*
> *And the creed and the colour and the name won't matter,*
> *were you there?'*

Sydney Carter

Lord, help me not just to say yes, but do it—now.

CHAPTER 8

Day in, day out

PHILIPPIANS 4:13

I can do all things through him who strengthens me.

There I was, stuck in the front row of a church with a group of other young people, and trying desperately not to be noticed. Not because I am naturally shy and retiring, but because of what I was wearing. A white dress, made out of parachute silk with pennies sewn in around the bottom to keep it from flying over my head— but making me look like an overgrown flower fairy. On my head a white veil, for I was a confirmation candidate, and a white dress and veil were still standard dress for girls to wear at confirmation. My mother had been delighted to obtain the parachute silk, as it meant she had not had to part with any of those precious clothing coupons, and a friend had offered to make up the dress free of charge. I was not happy in it! All I wanted to do was get out of that church, go home and change into something more normal. Most of the other candidates were still at school, but I had left school at fourteen and was in my first job, as an apprentice cook. I felt out of place, out of sorts, and certainly out of fashion.

Suddenly I was jolted out of my own thoughts by the words, 'I can do all things through Christ who strengthens me.' I looked up and saw the Bishop standing in the pulpit. He had grabbed my attention, and seemed to be looking at me too. He repeated the sentence, as if he knew I had not really heard it the first time. He went on, 'Christ is like dynamite, and can change your life, if you will let him', but as he continued his sermon I lost interest, and returned to worrying about my outfit, hoping none of my friends would see me in it. Then again came those words, 'I can do all things through Christ who strengthens me. Always remember that, won't you?' With that parting shot, the Bishop finished his sermon, and we went on to sing the next hymn. But I could not get those words out of my mind. Was it true? Could you do anything through Christ? More to the point, could I? I decided that for someone like me it was a fairly remote possibility. It was all right for someone at the Grammar School, going on to college or university, or for those who had fashion sense and the figure to go with it, but surely not me, and anyway, what did it mean by 'all things'? Making a fortune, piloting a plane, travelling the world, owning a company, speaking a foreign language, becoming a Member of Parliament...? I began to indulge in a flight of fancy, especially regarding the Member of Parliament bit, because I did have political ambition. I really did want to do something about the world I lived in, to make it better—'fair shares for all'—but the dream was not likely to become a reality, not for someone like me.

The following Sunday, when thankfully I had managed to pack away that dress (although my mother had looked at it and said, 'It might come in for another time...'), I went to church and received my first communion. Afterwards our vicar presented those of us who had been confirmed with a prayer book. The boys received a blue one entitled 'A prayer book for men and boys', the girls a red one, 'A prayer book for women and girls'. I never did find out whether the instructions contained in the two varied much, but they were all inscribed with our names, the date and place of our confirmation, and that text, 'I can do all things through Christ who strengthens me' (Philippians 4:13) and underneath, 'Christ, my dynamite'. After that Sunday the dress went up into the loft, I went back to my work as an apprentice cook, and the book went in the drawer beside my bed. From time to time I would read it, think about what I read, try to put into practice some of those instructions for leading a good Christian life, but nothing much happened—not for several years, anyway. Yet that verse was always there in my mind, and the question, 'Could it be true?' was food for thought as I worked away in the canteen kitchen. Looking back now, I know that a seed was sown that night. It took time to germinate, even longer to put its head above the surface, but I am sure that I owe more than I can ever repay to the one who spoke those words so clearly and with such assurance. I would like to say I remembered his sermon, but that would be untrue. Just the text, and that phrase 'Christ is like dynamite   '

Is it true? I have not made a fortune, piloted a plane or travelled the world (only parts of it). I do not own a company, or speak any foreign languages, nor have I become a Member of Parliament—the nearest has been working as Chaplain to the Chairman of the Selby District Council—but I have discovered and experienced the reality of those words in a far more dramatic, exciting and rewarding way than I could have done by fulfilling any of those flights of fancy.

I have also had the joy and privilege of seeing so many people accomplishing the seemingly impossible, attaining heights beyond imagining, being agents of transformation, endeavour, service, scholarship, ministry and mission, through Christ. Going into places and situations no one else would have dared to go, and yet in the power of Jesus Christ bringing healing and hope, comfort and dignity, to those who seemed beyond the reach of God or human help. I see it happening before my eyes, and I am bowled over by it all. Is it true? A million times more so than I could have begun even to dare think possible.

But there is even more to it than this. A dimension of 'all things' which is seen in the depths of suffering and endurance, confusion and doubt. A young mother cares for a terribly disabled child. It is a 'round the clock' responsibility giving her little time for anything else, yet she has formed a support group to help others in a similar situation. She is always ready with advice and encouragement. Providing a shoulder to cry on, an ear to listen, she says, 'I know Jesus is with me, and he gives me the strength I need.' An elderly lady makes the journey each day to be with her husband who has Alzheimer's, and is now in care. She had a number of years at home when he was violent towards her, destructive, demanding; and yet she never stopped loving and caring for him. Now, for his safety and hers, he is in care, but she goes to see him so cheerfully and excitedly like a young bride. She takes him his favourite cakes, reads to him, shares family news, sitting holding his hand. The love she has for him is so evident, and yet there is no response, no welcome, no signs of recognition. She says, 'I don't see what others see, I see the man I love, and I will always love him.' How does she cope? She smiles, 'The Lord is good, he knows, he understands, and one day he will make it right.'

A young man, now in a wheelchair, had to take 'retirement' from the work he so enjoyed, in his early thirties. Over the past few years he had felt increasingly God's call to ministry, but it seemed impossible as his health deteriorated. He held fast to his calling, however, and travelled by public transport once a week to Sheffield to study evangelism. Now he has been accepted for training as a

Church Army Officer, and he, his wife and two youngsters look forward eagerly to the new life ahead. As he has gone forward in faith he has grown in leaps and bounds in confidence, skills and ability. Still in a wheelchair, yes, but we do not notice the wheelchair, we see what God can do with someone who takes him at his word. He is an inspiration to all who come in contact with him, a challenge to those who say, 'But I couldn't do that...'

A very gifted forty-year-old wife and mother, with a real talent and vision for helping and leading young people, has a progressing asthmatic condition, which now means she is unable to exercise her gifts because she is confined almost entirely to her home and, for long periods, to her bed. She struggled with all this, not least with the question of why, if the Lord had given her these gifts and the vision to use them, was she prevented from using them? She has grown in her faith, in a positive acceptance of her situation, and in her joy in the Lord each day. She has a confidence in God's plan and purpose, even though she cannot see what it is, and even though every possibility seems to be thwarted.

Another young man suffers from periods of deep depression, and in spite of times when he seems at last to be free of it, it seems to return with a greater intensity. Even in this he can testify to knowing that however he feels or however dark the situation appears, the Lord is there, and will bring him through—'the hand in the darkness,' as he puts it.

All these people, and they are but a tiny sample of others like them, know by experience what Paul means when he writes of being able to 'do all things through him who strengthens me'—the strength that comes from acceptance and contentment in good times and bad. Paul was a 'go-getter' for the Lord. So much talent, enthusiasm, power, always striving to reach new heights in sharing the good news of Jesus Christ, yet not naturally the sort of person who would be patient, accepting and forgiving—and this comes out in his letters. He so often harangues those who are falling into error, misunderstanding what the faith is about, failing to get on with others or seeming slow in pushing forward. Imagine what it must have been like at times to be in his company! Yet he suffered greatly, not least by being imprisoned and so unable to continue his travelling. He also suffered what he describes as 'a thorn in the flesh', which he found difficult and restricting—and he makes no bones about that, for he writes about appealing to the Lord for the removal of his problem. Then the answer comes, 'But he said to me, "My grace is sufficient for you, for power is made perfect in weakness". So, I will boast all the more gladly of my weaknesses, so that the power of Christ may dwell in me. Therefore I am content with weaknesses, insults, hardships, persecutions, and calamities for the sake of Christ; for whenever I am weak, then I am strong' (2 Corinthians 12:9–10).

John Holmes, in his book *When I am Weak*, writes about this paradox of strength and weakness:

> *Weakness is part of our experience as Christians. Not just the weakness of sin, but also the weakness of suffering, of failure, of fear and depression, even despair. Yet such weakness will not overwhelm us if we are able to face it with the grace of Christ … To acknowledge our weakness is so often the breakthrough. To acknowledge weakness to ourselves, and to God can lead to a fresh awareness of his grace.*

I see that being lived out in the lives of so many the world pities or passes by, and yet they are the strong, the free and the really content people. I look at them, and stand in awe and amazement, and wonder how I would cope with even a tiny amount of what they have to cope with, day in, day out. Like Paul, I prefer the all-action, on-the-go sort of life, yet when at times I have been forced by circumstances to accept weakness, even admit it to others, I have found a strength, a peace and acceptance I would not have believed possible in me. I dare not say with Paul, 'I have learned to be content with whatever I have'—but I am learning, and I know this: having that sense of contentment makes everything else fall into place, day in, day out, and will continue to do so until one day when all will be revealed!

I am no longer my own, but thine.
Put me to what thou wilt, rank me with whom thou wilt.
Put me to doing, put me to suffering,
let me be employed for thee, or laid aside for thee.

Let me be full, let me be empty,
let me have all things, let me have nothing.
I freely and heartily yield all things to thy pleasure and disposal.

(Part of the Act of Dedication from the Methodist Covenant Service)

Lord,
For all things I thank you,
in all things I trust you,
through all things may I know
your peace and your victory—
and so be content.

CHAPTER 9

Take a good look

I SAMUEL 16:7

The Lord does not see as mortals see; they look on the outward appearance, but the Lord looks on the heart.

The search for a king was over, or so Samuel thought as he looked at Eliab, the oldest son of Jesse. Tall and handsome, the obvious choice—but God saw what lay within that man, what was at the heart of him, and it was not the heart of a king. At the end of the day it was the youngest son, David, the lad looking after the sheep, who was chosen, because Samuel heeded God's word, and saw the qualities needed for kingship in a boy. It would have been so easy to go on first impressions and to have made a disastrous appointment, but Samuel was enabled to see the true picture, the potential of the one who would become the great King David.

We all jump to conclusions so quickly, go by first impressions, base our decisions on the immediate and outward appearance. In our minds we sum up another person in seconds by how we see them at that moment, their colouring, their stance, the clothes they are wearing, their accent. Appearances can be very deceptive, but so often we do not learn, because we do not give the time to discover what lies beneath the exterior. Samuel saw seven candidates before David. He had learned the value of waiting, looking, and seeing.

In the play *A Raisin in the Sun* by Lorraine Hansberry, the character Mama says this: 'Whenever you start measuring somebody, measure him right, child, measure him right. Make sure you done taken into account what hills and valleys he came through before he got to wherever he is.'

What have been the influences, the opportunities, the disadvantages, the handicaps that a person has had, and what has that person done with them? Life throws all sorts of things at us, but it is how we receive and use them that makes us the person we are inside. As the action of the heart dictates the body, so our character is formed by the responses of our spirit, either negatively or positively.

Each year in Selby Abbey a special service is held for carers and those they care for, and it is always such a happy occasion, a real inspiration to be there. So I was delighted to be sharing in it again this year. I had seen the boy in his chair earlier, before the service began. I had only given him a quick glance, but realized he was obviously physically handicapped. Small, pale, with a rather lopsided expression, I unconsciously registered him in my mind as having learning difficulties too. Yet when I took his hand and spoke to him he responded with such an infectious smile that I realized he was far more aware than I had at first thought.

At the end of the service, as I was leaving, I found myself beside the boy and Kitty, one of the organizers of the service. She put her arm round the boy and said, 'Right then, my little friend, we will go and have a cup of tea.' To which the boy replied in a strong, firm voice, 'I am not your little friend, I am your Prince Charming, and I am going to gallop away with you on my horse to my castle, and there I will make all your dreams come true, and give you your heart's desire.' That had me stopped in my tracks. I leaned over to Kitty and said, 'There's an offer too good to be refused!' I was then introduced to Timothy, and found out quite a lot more about him. Disabled in many ways, yes, but inside there is a strong, lively, caring and discerning young man. Because of his disabilities he is unable to go to school, and he has to spend much of his life in hospital, totally dependent on others, but what a character, what a joy to meet! He is indeed a Prince Charming in the truest sense, and brings such joy to everyone he meets.

As I drove home I said to myself, 'You see, Margaret, you jump to conclusions, you were wrong again—a good job you got a second chance to meet that remarkable young man. Try and remember that next time!'

The Timothys of this world have so much to give, rather like that young shepherd boy, David, who also might have been overlooked had not Samuel been given the gift of discernment by God, and used it.

One of the popular expressions of today is, 'What you see is what you get,' meaning of course that everything is open and above board, all there to be seen, with nothing hidden. An advertisement I saw recently made a very clever play on those words to introduce a new car. It read, 'What you see is not all you get', implying that this model was well worth a second look, for it had some very attractive hidden extras, a bargain not to be missed. Maybe something to bear in mind when we look at people and we think we see the whole picture. But what lies beneath the surface of our lives? Would we like it to be seen, or are we rather ashamed of parts of our personality, those deep hidden recesses? Do we try to cover them up, disguise them, hope no one sees that side of us?

Jesus had strong words of warning to those who do that. He saw through their disguise, saying to them, 'Woe to you, scribes and Pharisees, hypocrites! For you are like whitewashed tombs, which on the outside look beautiful, but inside they are full of the bones of the dead and of all kinds of filth. So you also on the outside look righteous to others, but inside you are full of hypocrisy and lawlessness' (Matthew 23:27–28). We may not be scribes or Pharisees, but maybe we do play-act, which is what hypocrisy is—acting a part, rather than being ourselves. An old saying has it: 'You can fool all of the people some of the time, and some of the people all of the time, but you can't fool all of the people all of the time'—and we can't fool God any of the time! God knows about the parts of our lives of which we are ashamed, which we wish were different. If we are honest with him, he will forgive us and enable us to be the people he wants us to be, the people we want to be. He sees our heart, understands our weaknesses, and if we genuinely want to be different he is there for us. We can pray as the psalmist did, 'Create in me a clean heart, O God, and put a new and right spirit within me' (Psalm 51:10) and know that God will hear and answer. At the end of the day it is what God knows and not what other people think that really matters. We have no need to play games, pretend, or cover up, but we must be open and honest, willing to be changed. In this way we will discover our true identity.

> *O for a heart to praise my God,*
> *a heart from sin set free,*
> *a heart that's sprinkled with the blood,*
> *so freely shed for me.*
> *Thy nature, gracious Lord, impart,*
> *come quickly from above.*
> *Write thy new name upon my heart,*
> *thy new best name of love.*

Charles Wesley, 1707–1788

CHAPTER 10

When you pray

LUKE 11:1-4

*He was praying in a certain place, and after he had finished,
one of his disciples said to him, 'Lord, teach us to pray, as John
taught his disciples.' He said to them, 'When you pray, say:
Father, hallowed be your name. Your kingdom come. Give us each
day our daily bread. And forgive us our sins, for we ourselves
forgive everyone indebted to us. And do not bring us
to the time of trial.'*

My first week at the senior school, and the first art class. The
teacher had told us to do a drawing or painting of whatever we
liked, so as to get the feel of the art room and its facilities, and no
doubt so she could get an idea of our abilities or signs of promise.
I gazed at the blank piece of paper. It did not challenge me, rather
it leered at me, reminding me of my lack of talent or imagination.
I noticed my neighbour was busily sketching out a figure, and I
watched in admiration as she brought that figure to life, with confident, swift strokes. When the class finished I leaned over and
asked, 'Can I have a look, please?' She showed it to me, a magnificent drawing of one of my favourite characters, Mickey Mouse!
'How do you do that?' She looked at me in surprise, 'Oh, it's easy,
I've always been able to do it.' 'Could you show me how to?' She
picked up a piece of paper and again began to draw, but this time
more slowly and definitely as I watched. The she said, 'You have a
go now.' I tried, not very successfully, but then the next effort was
a bit better. I felt excited, 'I can draw Mickey Mouse!' She gave me
the piece of paper with her drawing on it. 'It comes easy with practice,' she told me encouragingly, and that day I not only learned
how to draw Mickey Mouse, but made a new friend. Over the years
I have amused countless children, including our own, with my
drawings of Mickey Mouse, and basked in their admiration. When
I am bored in meetings, as sometimes I am, I amuse myself by
drawing Mickey Mouse on agendas, doodling around on the edges
of notice papers—it helps concentrate the mind so nicely! I picked
up my old autograph book this week, which I began at the age of

twelve and continued until my late teens. There on one page is a pen-and-ink drawing of Mickey Mouse, with name and date, 'B Naylor 4 2 46'. I wonder what happened to her, and whether she kept up her drawing? I can't remember what any of the teachers taught me at that school, but I still remember and practise what Barbara inspired me to do, through seeing her bring that character to life.

It has been said that the greatest lessons in life are 'caught, not taught'—seeing the effect in another person's life, be it academic or sporting achievements, or a particular hobby or vocation that has transformed their life, fired them and inspired others to catch the vision and follow in their footsteps. Our son, a well-known and successful fisherman, author of several books on the subject, column writer, specialist in his field, was inspired to take up the hobby when he was a schoolboy, through meeting and watching a fisherman who took him under his wing, taught him how to fish and encouraged him to develop his talent. 'Caught not taught' is not completely true, however. We need to be caught first, and inspired, and then we will be willing and eager to be taught, to learn for ourselves, so as to enjoy the delights of our master's experience.

Mickey Mouse, the art of fishing, and praying come into that category! Why did the disciples ask Jesus to teach them to pray? After all, from childhood they had learned to pray, and prayer was a way of life for every Jew. Prayers for every moment, every occasion. Set forms, times and places. Prayer was not an option, but a duty to be performed in accordance with the law. A visit to the Holy Land brought home to me how important this is for modern-day religious Jews too. As soon as I boarded the aircraft I saw Jews at prayer. Then, in the arrival lounge, in Tel Aviv, on the way into Jerusalem, and at every corner, on every street, there were people praying. To see the prayer area in front of the Western Wall in Jerusalem filled with those praying, rocking figures, and the sounds rising and filling the surrounding area reminded me of why that wall is called 'the Wailing Wall'. Together with the frequent calls to prayer from the mosques, the sight of Muslims at prayer, prostrating themselves, and the Christian pilgrimage groups wending their way along the Via Dolorosa singing, praying, chanting in many different languages, made me realize why Jerusalem is indeed the

Holy City— it is sacred to all three of the world's great religions, Judaism, Christianity, and Islam, and to pray there is the desire of people of all faiths.

The disciples of Jesus were steeped in prayer, but they saw in Jesus something outside their own practice and understanding. They observed him at prayer, recognized how much he needed and delighted in it. The strength he derived, the joy, the assurance and the resolution it gave him, were an expression not just of traditional words and posture, but of a relationship, as intimate as a son with his father. The disciples caught the vision of prayer by seeing it in action, lived out in the life of Jesus. When he spoke to them of the need for prayer they recognized that what he showed and taught was of a different dimension altogether, compared to what they knew. John the Baptist had taught his followers simple prayers, and some of the disciples had been followers of John and would have known and used the prayers he had taught, and so they ask Jesus to teach them in the same way. You can almost see the group of disciples sitting quietly watching Jesus praying, looking at his face, his 'body language', realizing they were party to something very special, very holy, and longing to share it. Then as he turns to them they ask him to teach them to pray like that. So he tells them, 'When you pray, say: Father, hallowed be your name...' and he then continues with what has come to be known as the Lord's Prayer. In the account of Matthew's Gospel it comes in the context of the Sermon on the Mount, when Jesus tells them first what prayer is not, about the misuse of prayer, and then goes on, 'Pray then in this way: Our Father in heaven...' (Matthew 6:9). In both instances he is responding to his disciples, his followers, and that prayer in various forms has come down through the last two thousand years. It is the prayer that unifies Christian people. Sadly we may not be able to join in holy communion with all our Christian brothers and sisters, but we can all share in 'the prayer our Saviour taught us'. I prefer using the traditional form, because it is the form which I was taught as a child, and which my husband Peter and I use each day together in our prayers, which we have followed throughout our married life, shared with our children and helped others to use. It is still the form most widely known and used, and I am all for unity.

But whether it is sung, said, chanted in whatever language or version, it is still our Lord's prayer, his gift to us. It is the perfect prayer, for it begins with giving God the glory, affirming his sovereign will. Then we bring our needs to him, putting everything into his hands. William Barclay, writing on the Lord's Prayer in his commentary on the Gospel of Matthew, says,

> *God is first given his supreme place, and then and only then, we turn to ourselves and our needs and desires. It is only when God is given his proper place that all other things fall into their proper places... but not only is this a prayer which brings the whole of life to the presence of God, it is also a prayer which brings the whole of God to our lives.*

It is for all times, all situations, all places. It is a wonderful sight to see children with their eyes tightly closed, their hands together, saying that prayer. It is wonderful to be part of a vast gathering united in sharing it; in the 'rites of passage' at baptisms, weddings and funerals bringing ourselves before God our Father, who knows and loves us, and wills the very best for us. It is wonderful to hold someone's hand as they slip from this life into the next, mouthing those familiar words, which give them peace and confidence to make that journey into the knowledge of the kingdom, the power and the glory for ever and ever, and to reflect quietly by ourselves on those words which provide us too with 'something for the journey'.

Jesus had a unique relationship with God his father, of love and obedience. Because of that relationship he could trust his father in everything, however difficult and distressing. In the garden of Gethsemane Jesus prayed in such deep agony that his sweat was like blood, but he prayed with the simple trust of a small child with his dad. He called God 'Abba'—Daddy—and his prayer was 'Abba, Father, for you all things are possible; remove this cup from me; yet, not what I want, but what you want' (Mark 14:36). Perhaps that is the most difficult prayer for any of us to pray and yet through that prayer of obedience we too can call God 'Abba—Father'. We can learn to pray, find the joy of being attuned to our Father in heaven, and doing his will here on earth, for the two go together.

Michael Ramsey in his book *Be Still and Know* writes,

Christian prayer and Christian life are properly inseparable.
As the Sonship of Jesus on earth was a relation to the Father in
words, in wordless converse and in the obedience of a life and
death, so the adopted sonship of the Christians has its facets of
word, silence and act. The Sonship of Jesus was to the Father's
glory, and in the serving of that glory he consecrated himself on
the world's behalf.

So when we, his disciples of today, catch the vision, feel within us
the longing for that close relationship in prayer, we have to count
the cost of discipleship, of what it means to honestly and without
reserve pray the Lord's prayer, and to live it out in our lives. We
may feel fearful, inadequate, unprepared to dare utter those words,
but we need not be afraid, or hold back. Jesus leads us gently by
the hand into his and our Father's presence, gives us that nudge of
encouragement and as we fumble around hardly daring to breathe,
let alone speak, yet wanting so desperately to give ourselves to him
in love as Jesus did, he whispers to us, 'When you pray, say:
Father...' Once we have said that, and know that, we are at one in
heaven and on earth. The door to God is wide open, and he wel-
comes us in, as his beloved children, to share in his eternal and
loving purpose.

As our Saviour has taught us, so we pray,

'Our Father, who art in heaven, hallowed be thy name.
Thy kingdom come. Thy will be done, on earth as it is in heaven.
Give us this day our daily bread, and forgive us our trespasses,
as we forgive those who trespass against us.
And lead us not into temptation, but deliver us from evil.
For thine is the kingdom, the power and the glory,
for ever and ever. Amen.'

Lord, teach us to pray, and help us never to be
afraid of the answer.

CHAPTER 11

The shepherd & his sheep

PSALM 23:1-3

*The Lord is my shepherd, I shall not want. He makes me
lie down in green pastures; he leads me beside still waters; he
restores my soul. He leads me in right paths for his name's sake.*

He stood there in the field, leaning on his stick, his dog crouched
beside him. Both of them motionless, apart from their eyes darting
here and there, observing the grazing sheep, the bouncing lambs
who were chasing each other across the field, until recalled by their
mothers' anxious 'baa, baa'.

Now and again a small lamb would suddenly discover it had lost
sight of its mother, and would bleat plaintively until a sheep, raising its head and recognizing the sound of its lamb, plodded across,
and a joyful reunion would take place, the lamb latching on to the
'milk on tap' and its mother resuming her grazing. An ordinary
everyday sight up in the Yorkshire Dales in late spring. The green
fields and hills covered in white dots—hundreds of sheep and
their lambs enjoying the warm sunshine, the abundant grass, the
keen fresh air.

Up the lane came more sheep and lambs with their shepherd
and his dog, the cars behind them patiently waiting, accepting that
in the Dales sheep have priority, and anyway, there was no chance
of passing on that narrow lane. It was a matter of tagging on behind
until the gate was opened into the field, the sheep driven in to their
new pastures, and the shepherd turned, giving a cheery wave of
acknowledgment to the drivers, before following his charges across
the field.

The stuff of picture postcards, and much photographed by visitors to the Dales at this time of year with their cameras at the ready
to capture country life, seen at its best. It is not always such an
idyllic scene, though. Only a few weeks beforehand the Dales had
been held in winter's icy grip. Days of heavy snow were followed
by torrential rain and gales, resulting in swollen rivers and flooded
fields, and the shepherds were hard pressed to cover the ground,
searching out sheep in trouble, sodden bundles stuck in hedges or

unable to get back to dry land. The injured, the frightened and the sick had to be carefully rescued, often carried in the arms of the shepherd to the road, for in such conditions even the best four-wheel-drive vehicles are useless. Even in summer the weather can turn nasty, and in the lambing season the shepherds are on alert twenty-four hours a day, caring for sheep having difficulties, lambs needing attention. And in bad weather many a Dales farmhouse kitchen has been home to bedraggled, frightened, newborn lambs, even the kitchen range ovens giving that vital boost to them, before they could return to their mothers in the field. It is not only the weather that can prove a danger—there has to be constant vigilance making sure gates are shut, hedges and fencing secure, walls kept in good repair, the streams and rivers inspected in case any lambs or sheep have fallen in, or are lying injured; and watch must be kept for sheep stealers, still a real problem for local farmers.

There is more, much more to being a shepherd than leaning on a stick in the sunshine! Shepherds are very special people. Most are born of generations of shepherds; it is in their blood, and there's nothing you can tell them about sheep and of all the endless variety needed in caring for them. Modern technology can be an enormous help in their work. I know of one shepherd who has closed-circuit television in his lambing sheds, and I am sure he is not the only one. Shepherds are to be seen driving across their fields on quad bikes, 'fetching and carrying' using the latest specialized vehicles, but what marks out a good shepherd is that vast store of wisdom in his head, and the loving concern in his heart, for his sheep. They know him, he knows them, and they bear his mark, for from birth they are marked by their owner's colour or number.

Whenever I see a shepherd, the words of the 23rd psalm come into my mind—words of David, the shepherd king, who I am sure would have been equally at home up here in the Dales as looking after his sheep in Israel, his training ground for kingship. When I visited the Holy Land several years ago, it was a special thrill for me to see the shepherds in their flowing robes and headdresses leading their sheep just as David must have done, an unchanged and unchanging occupation. David may have become the mighty king, writer and leader, but he always had the heart of a shepherd, the courage and wisdom that were so much part of being a shepherd, but which equipped him to care for people, to lead them, to make them strong. Yet he knew that he needed a master shepherd to care for him, to guide him, heal and protect him. His experiences as a shepherd drew out the picture of God as shepherd, a personal relationship with him, for he could say, 'The Lord is my shepherd, I shall not want.' Whatever happened, and David had a very chequered career, great highs and great lows, he knew that assurance of God's all-knowing, all-sustaining and all-loving care and concern in every aspect of his life. David's psalm touches a cord in everyone. It is said and sung probably more than any other psalm or hymn. Chosen to mark the beginning of life, often at baptism. A 'top of the pops' for weddings as couples set out on their life together, and again at the end of life's journey, in the funeral service. Words of assurance, comfort, strength, hope, trust. As I have sat with those in pain and distress by the bedside of the dying, and read to them the 23rd psalm, I have seen and felt the difference it has made. Often in their dying moments their lips frame those words, 'The Lord is my shepherd...'

Those words came to me as I was giving birth to our son, when there were fears for his life and for mine, and I felt almost paralysed by blind panic. As I said the words of the 23rd psalm I felt the presence of the Lord who was my shepherd holding me and our unborn child safe and secure, leading us through the dark valley into the light. Soon after, a very healthy 'lamb' was delivered, and his bleating cry was music to my ears, and to everyone else in that delivery room of the hospital in Bury, Lancashire. While outside a blizzard raged, public services were cut off and people were snowed in, we were safe and secure in the fold!

I had the same experience in the summer of 1997 in Italy, not giving birth to a child, I hasten to add, but sliding down a hillside of shale, one foot trapped underneath me, at an ever-gathering speed almost worthy of an Olympic skier—but without skis. As I hit the bottom and realized I had a useless and badly broken foot and ankle, and wondered how I was ever going to get help (for I was alone, having wandered off like a very silly sheep), I said to myself firmly those words, 'The Lord is my shepherd, I shall not want...' and felt again the assurance that he would restore me, body and soul, and that I would know goodness and mercy even in that situation. Looking back now on that event, and on all that came afterwards—the care and kindness both in Italy and on arriving back in this country, the spell in the York District Hospital, the skill of those who put my foot together again, and the healing that followed—the love that surrounded me through a fairly long and difficult time was yet another instance of knowing in an even deeper way the reality of those words.

Those are two extreme instances, giving birth and an accident, but the 23rd psalm is for me a well used and much loved affirmation of my shepherd's care at all times and in all places. He does not promise that everything will be easy, but he promises that even through the darkest times and places, 'the valley of the shadow of death', he is there, and he will take us safely through. How can we be sure of that? Look at Jesus! There we see our shepherd, who says to us, 'I am the good shepherd... and I lay down my life for the sheep.' He is and he did. Jesus gave his life so that we might live. He takes us through the shadows, through death itself, to the life he has prepared for us for eternity. Even the very best and bravest of human shepherds can lose a sheep or lamb, can fail to save it because of the situation it has got into, the prevailing conditions, the state of its injuries; but Jesus never loses one of his. Those who belong to him, marked as his by his cross, are safe for eternity. He is our Shepherd, our Saviour and our King. We will all pass through the shadows, through the darkness of death itself, but then out into the glorious light of the kingdom of heaven. Jesus takes personal responsibility for us, and even though we may stray and wander, get ourselves into all sorts of problems and difficulties, he will still reach out to us and bring us gently but firmly back. I know that only too well myself, and how grateful I am for his grip upon me!

'I am the good shepherd.' Words of confidence and assurance from cradle to grave and beyond, but also a challenge to us to listen to our shepherd's voice, to respond to his call, and obey his commands. If only we would do that then we would save ourselves a great deal of trouble, and others also!

Lord, Sheep can be very silly at times—they just ask for trouble.
They wander off, leave the safety of their field and
struggle through gaps, get entangled in the bushes, rush across
busy roads, just because they think there is something
more attractive further on, down there, away from the others.
Some don't think at all, just follow the others, even when
it is dangerous and foolhardy. But then sheep are sheep.
They don't know any better, do they?

People can be very silly at times—they just ask for trouble.
They wander off, get into trouble, follow the others.
Some are very weak, some a bit too clever for their own good,
others are just indifferent to help or advice, even to love
poured out for them. But then people are people. They don't know
any better, or do they?

'All we, like sheep, have gone astray...' All of us, me included,
following our own way, doing our own thing, wandering
off. Yet you love us, care about us, want the very best for us, and
reach out to us wherever we are, and whatever we have done.
What a good shepherd you are, how great is your power and your
love. Thank you for loving, following and saving me.

The King of love my shepherd is,
whose goodness faileth never,
I nothing lack if I am his,
and he is mine for ever.

Henry Williams Baker, 1821–1877

CHAPTER 12

Use your wings

ISAIAH 40:31

Those who wait for the Lord shall renew their strength,
they shall mount up with wings like eagles,
they shall run and not be weary, they shall walk and not faint.

I found them quite irresistible—compulsive viewing, you could say—watching those gliders so gracefully, noiselessly and, it seemed to me, effortlessly floating across the sky. Often they appeared to be motionless, before rising high, sweeping round like long-limbed ballet dancers, and then descending before disappearing out of sight to land at the small airfield just a couple of miles from our home. As I gazed up into the sky at them, I marvelled that something so small and flimsy could be capable of flight, and I was full of admiration for those who flew in them. 'It must be a lovely feeling up there, but what a long drop down!' I half promised myself, 'One day, I might...' but that was as far as it ever got! I would have loved to have had a go, but my feet were well and truly fixed on earth, where it seemed the most sensible place to keep them. My references to the joy of gliding met with wry smiles from my family, and jokes about 'one of mum's fads' and the query, 'You would never go up in one of those, would you?' to which I would say, 'One of these days I might surprise you.' This would provoke even more laughter, and I would rapidly change the subject.

Then one day it all came to a head. A lovely spring day, clear blue sky, and so we had decided to have a day at the coast. We had gone to Bridlington and we were walking across the top of the cliffs—my husband Peter, daughter Alison, and myself. I suddenly saw the glider, high in the sky, over the sea. It was so beautiful that I just stood there watching and admiring it. Peter and Alison had continued to walk along, and then, realizing I was no longer with them, turned and called out to me to come on. I pointed up to the glider. 'I'd love to be up there.' I got the usual response, and there and then my mind was made up. 'Right,' I said, 'I'll show you.'

Nothing more was said but the following day I got in touch with a gliding club near York who were advertising one-day courses, and asked them when there was one available. When I was told it was the following Saturday, I gulped, and then said, 'Do you take anybody, even an idiot woman of fifty?' The cheery reply was, 'We take anyone. Come along on Saturday.'

On the Saturday morning I announced, 'I'm going on a gliding course today.' My family's faces were a picture. Open-mouthed, they gazed at me, whether with horror or admiration I couldn't make out. 'You are not—you can't—can we come and watch?' I assured them I was going, it was fixed, and no they couldn't come! An hour later I was looking down at what seemed a very small and very fragile craft. Was it really capable of taking me up into the air— and even more of keeping me up there for a while? The instructor was a cheerful man. Strapping me in, he promised that there was nothing to worry about, and I would enjoy the experience. Being towed up by a small plane felt no different to any other take-off, but it was when the tow was released high in the sky that I felt the real freedom of gliding. I felt as free as a bird. Once I had got used to being airborne, the instructor gave me details of the glider and how to handle it, and after a while I was allowed to take the controls for a time before we began the descent, and much to my surprise and relief came smoothly down to earth.

It was one of those very special experiences, and maybe one day I will do it again, who knows. But at least I had done it! I couldn't get home quickly enough to recount my exploits. 'Did you really do it? Are you having us on?' Did I do it! I produced my receipt. This time they did not laugh, but patted me on the back. 'Well done.' The following day I told my colleague David about my day. 'You didn't think I would, did you?' He smiled, 'Oh yes, I did, I know you. If you say you will, then you will!'

That of course was sixteen years ago now and, no, I have not done it again. I have not felt the need or desire, but when I look up at the sky now and see the gliders, I can say, 'I know what it's like, I have been there!' Anyway, I have a few more 'One day I will…'s tucked away to be brought out at the right time!

I suppose all of us have our daydreams about what we would like to do 'one day', the plans we make 'for later on, when we have more time… when the children are grown up… when we retire…' Gradually the dreams fade, and there is a sadness that we did not take the opportunities that were there, but we feel it is too late, and that attitude remains with us, and can spoil our enjoyment and effectiveness today. At fifty I was beginning to think the time for adventure was running out. Fifty was a time for questioning, looking back, and realizing that so many things I had thought 'one day...' might not now be possible. So for me that day's gliding course made all the difference. It proved to me that you can do something entirely different, that others might think is beyond you. Something that has just been a hazy aspiration even in your own mind is obtainable, and so can be a spur to adventures in the future, releasing you to be open to the challenges that might be presented, at whatever age they come.

Francis Dewar in his book *Give Yourself a Break* says this: 'For their soul's health, everyone needs an opportunity now and then to take wings and fly, to do something that gives expression to the gift that is in them which is not called forth in their ordinary life and work...' I like that! In my case it was actually taking wings and flying, but it is far more than that. It is a spiritual experience, putting into practice what God offers us, to be free to be ourselves, to be different, to be renewed. To fly in the face of our own inhibitions, and the discouragements of others.

I am constantly meeting people of all ages who wistfully tell me of things they might have done, places they could have gone to, plans that never got off the drawing board, to which I say, 'But what is stopping you now?' Of course for a few it is too late, although in many cases with a bit of adaptation they could in part fulfil their dreams. For most though, it is a case of other things taking over that space, eating up their resources (I do not just mean financial— that often is the least of the problems), and of allowing demands to displace dreams.

The prophet Joel writes of the time when God's Spirit will be poured out on all, young and old, men and women, and even on slaves—and we all allow ourselves to become enslaved to the world, to its demands, to public and personal opinion. The word that comes through Joel, 'Your sons and daughters shall prophesy, your old men shall dream dreams, and your young men shall see visions' (Joel 2:28), is equally for us today, for God's Spirit has been poured out, is here and now, if only we would realize it, be open to it, rejoice in it! What use are dreams and visions if we do nothing about them, if they remain fixed firmly here on earth, on ourselves and our limitations and inhibitions? God's Spirit is a liberating, empowering Spirit, and for all who will welcome the Spirit, those dreams and visions can become glorious realities, a means of discovering more of God's purposes, experiencing more of his glory.

Today every organization, business undertaking, voluntary society, and church has a 'mission statement'. Discussed and debated, amended and extended, honed and tuned until finally there it is in black and white—or sometimes in wonderful multicolour: the mission statement. I am delighted to see aims and objectives so clearly defined, the purpose so succinctly set out, and I am quite sure these add so much to the thinking out and planning of operations, keeping the essential ethos before the membership. But what really counts is whether or not those aims and objectives are operative, whether they have ever got off the ground, taking effect. Where is the evidence? It is one thing to have written down, 'The committee were unanimous in deciding we should...' quite another to get people to do it! At the end of the day those dreams and visions have to take off, have a life, become reality. Once that happens then more will follow, it will begin to flow and grow, achieve its purpose. We need to be challenged, even goaded into action.

I have always loved those words from Isaiah 40 pointed out to me by a friend when I first became a Christian, reminding me of the need to 'wait for the Lord', to keep close to him in my daily life, so that I might be enabled to do what he had called me to do, be what he had called me to be. Perhaps, though, it took me to the age of fifty before I quite realized that God does not expect us to go on waiting for ever, or dreaming, or even having visions, but to put them into action! I have not ventured up in a glider since the age of fifty, but I have through that experience been encouraged to 'try my wings' in many other situations, and have found freedom and joy in discovering whole new worlds of opportunity. As some words of a hymn put it, praying, 'Lift my earthbound longings, fix them, Lord, above. Draw me with the magnet of thy mighty love' (William Walsham How, 1823–1897).

Lord, thank you that you draw us to adventures through dreams and visions, awaken us to the possibilities, help us to see beyond our own capabilities to what you want us to be and do for you, and by your Holy Spirit accomplish the same.

CHAPTER 13

Everything in season

ECCLESIASTES 3:1

For everything there is a season, and a time for every matter under heaven.

There they were, inviting me to reach out and put them into my shopping trolley. They looked as though they had come straight out of the pages of a catalogue, just perfect. Bright red, perfectly shaped, luscious lovely strawberries. Eve was tempted by a fruit in the garden of Eden and I knew the feeling! But this was no forbidden fruit, it was there for the taking—at a price. I decided that although they were so tempting, the price was not. They were far too expensive. Reluctantly I turned away and carried on with the more mundane, everyday sort of shopping. I looked through the windows, out into the car park. It was raining hard, a dismal winter's day in February, not the brightest of months. I made my mind up: I would have the strawberries as a treat for tea. Expensive, yes, but strawberries in February were well worth paying out for.

Having also got a carton of cream to go with the strawberries I headed towards the checkout. The operator smiled at me as she put through the strawberries and cream, 'Treating yourself?' I nodded. 'Bit dear, aren't they, but worth it? Nice to have a treat.' I agreed with her as I paid the bill, and made my way out into the rain, carefully protecting my precious package.

I felt very pleased with myself as I dished up the strawberries and cream that evening. 'I thought we would have something special, and they looked so good,' I said to Peter, not mentioning of course how much they had cost. We sat and ate them in silence. Neither of us spoke, but I knew we were both thinking the same thing—they were tasteless! I have a feeling the common carrot might have had more flavour. I had to admit I had made a mistake: 'They don't really taste of anything. They looked so good, but then you can't expect them to taste like the ones we pick ourselves. There's nothing like having things in their proper season.' I thought of summer as I said that, days picking strawberries in the fields nearby. The smell of them rising up from the earth, the softness and the flavour, summer teas, and at a price that didn't break the bank. They were worth waiting for. The expensive 'out of season' ones were not a patch on what in a few months would be in plentiful supply.

Walking round the supermarket this week I noticed that not only were there plenty of strawberries on display—and I managed to pass them by—but every variety of fruit and vegetable. A far cry from the days when we waited anxiously and excitedly for things to come into season—and how good they tasted. Those first new potatoes, the runner beans, raspberries, blackcurrants, lettuce, tomatoes and yes, the strawberries! For many things a short season, but how we enjoyed their season! We looked forward to them. We made the most of it when they came, and then, well, there was always the humble cabbage and rhubarb! Waiting for things used to be so much part of life, and maybe saying this is a sign of my increasing age. We were none the worse for having to wait. Saving up for new clothes, something for the home, a day out. Life had a zest, a sense of anticipation, and an acceptance of limitations.

The seasons of the year had a sharp distinction, marked out by unspoken rules. Even games in the schoolyard had their seasons; they weren't written down or announced, but they just happened, we all accepted that they did, and entered into them with great enthusiasm. Life itself was marked out by seasons, and by waiting time too. People fell in love then just as now, but there was an understood time of waiting, of preparation. Until the wedding they 'saved themselves'. Of course there were those who did not wait, but most did, and were glad they did too. A 'white wedding' was not just an outfit, but a statement of purity, of waiting, of giving to each other at the right time, in love. Death too was accepted, not in a blind, fatalistic way, but with serenity and with, in so many, a trust in God and faith in the future. The dying person was surrounded by family and friends, and usually in their own home. The body was not rushed away but remained at home until the funeral, visited, surrounded with loving care, still part of the family. Death was a fact of life.

Life was dictated by the seasons, and the words from Ecclesiastes set the tone of daily life and experience, like the regular, sweet tick-tock of the clock in the hall, or the solemn marking of the hours by the church bells.

Time today is more of an enemy than a friend. Getting from 'a' to 'b' is a question of doing the journey as fast as possible 'to save time', rather than giving time to appreciate something of the journey, travelling comfortably and safely, with regard not only to ourselves but the other road users. I have to plead guilty myself, as often I shoot out at the last possible minute, muttering at the sedate driver in front, or getting impatient when I am held up by roadworks. I have not yet succumbed to a mobile phone, though. I have been put off by the worried-looking characters walking along deep in conversation on the phone or, even worse, by those who use them on trains. I questioned one fellow traveller about the value of mobile phones on trains and he said, 'It's a question of making the best use of your time.' I was tempted to quote from Ecclesiastes '…a time to keep silence, and a time to speak…' but then decided maybe it was my time to keep silence, and try to be a bit more gracious about those who have to work every available moment, even on public transport.

While timepieces have become more and more sophisticated—just look at the variety of watches and clocks these days—I sometimes feel they are chains that enslave us, rather than gentle reminders of the value of each minute, the gift of time. What is lacking is the rhythm of life, the ebb and flow. Nowadays it's 'all go'.

As I read that third chapter of the book of Ecclesiastes—and I read through it quite often as a way of meditating, of getting myself centred again—I feel my balance being restored. It brings life into perspective, and I would recommend it as a very helpful practice. It is not only a picture of time, but also of timelessness, and it all falls into place in verse 11, which in the RSV reads, 'He (God) has made everything beautiful in its time; also he has put eternity into man's mind, yet so that he cannot find out what God has done from the beginning to the end' (Ecclesiastes 3:11). There is a time, a season for everything, and although it may be a much used and perhaps at times ill-used expression, 'God's timing is always right'. After all, God sent his son 'at the right time' and that was perfect timing, not just in time but in eternity. Our problem as human beings is that we get our sense of timing out of all proportion when we think and act in terms of this life, rather than in the light of eternity. With our ceaseless activity and anxiety we drown out that eternity dimension. When that happens we also lose out on the beauty of times and seasons, the 'now'. We clutch at straws rather than holding on to the hand of God.

In David Adam's book *Tides and Seasons* he speaks about the rhythms of creation, which have their parallels in our spiritual lives. He says, 'There is no doubt that we are caught up in cosmic, if not universal tides and seasons. We cannot control them all, nor can we stand apart, but we can seek to be more receptive and aware.'

Earlier this week I made my escape from the chains of time—just for a day! I had experienced several very difficult and demanding weeks of intense strain, most of it through my own fault, trying to push too much into too short a time, but also through several emergency situations which were thrust upon me. I knew it was 'make or break' and I fled to my hiding-place, over the North Yorkshire Moors to a spot overlooking the sea, at Whitby. I sat on a seat inscribed 'Captain R.G. Rippon 1914–1996' and the words, 'He would often rest about here.' I wondered who he was, but I thanked God that he had enjoyed resting there, as I now did, and thanked God too for those who had known him, and provided for others to enjoy what he had in his lifetime. I sat there for a long time just looking out to sea, watching the tide coming in fast and furious, but so beautiful and majestic, the sight and the smell of the sea ordering me, 'Sit there, just watch, breathe, be!' As I relaxed there I felt the strains and stresses of the last few weeks falling into place, easing, almost as though the sea had chased them away, the sea breezes blowing them up and away from me. Later on, I strolled round the harbour, looked at the boats, enjoyed a meal of fish and chips—a must at Whitby—and then walked along the top of the grassy path almost to Sandsend (the next place along the coast), before retracing my steps and returning for a last 'sit down' on the Captain's seat. By then the tide had turned, gentle now, leaving behind the golden, smooth-washed sands. Ebbing away quietly, in its own time, at its own determined pace. The last vestige of my tensions and anxiety ebbing away with the tide. 'Take life at a proper pace,' I told myself as I got into my car. 'Take a lesson from the sea!' Time well spent, time enjoyed, time to be. Time, no longer an enemy, but a friend, and now it was time to go home.

Father of all time and eternity, help me to rediscover through the light and darkness, the changing seasons, the ebb and flow of the sea, the natural rhythm of life. A way of life set free from the slavish worship of the human time-clock. To give myself space, so you can yet again remind me of your gift—and glory— of eternity, and in the light of that live in peace and harmony with you, the world and myself.

CHAPTER 14

But what do you say?

MATTHEW 16:13–16

*Now when Jesus came into the district of Caesarea Philippi,
he asked his disciples, 'Who do people say that the Son of Man
is?' And they said, 'Some say John the Baptist, but others
Elijah, and still others Jeremiah or one of the prophets.' He said
to them, 'But who do you say that I am?' Simon Peter
answered, 'You are the Messiah, the Son of the living God.'*

It takes, on average, three years to complete a full-time degree
course at university. Setting out as a student, leaving home maybe
for the first time, to a new area, different environment, away from
the security of home and family, familiar faces and places, it will be
an exciting yet daunting prospect. After the initial few weeks, most
settle down, get on with that new life, working hard (or not, as the
case may be), making new discoveries, new friends, taking up
interests and activities. Maybe they get a part-time job to help with
the cash flow, spend endless time drinking coffee—or something
stronger—and putting the world to rights, and during all this
getting to grips with the course, writing essays, going to tutorials,
listening to lectures, reading books, taking part in seminars, perhaps going out on a placement, getting practical experience. All the
time in the world, until the realization that time is running out!
Revision, panic, more revision, despair, more revision, more panic,
desperation, a glimmer of light, more revision, final examinations,
collapse, despair, hope, result! Degree day, proud parents, degree
awarded, celebrations, and now out into the big wide world, to discover if those three years have equipped you to begin a career, take
up an appointment, advance up the ladder, and fulfil your hopes
and the expectations of those who helped you along the way. Did
those three years give you anything more than a piece of paper, the
opportunity to put some letters behind your name? For that is what
it is all about: what you do with it.

Jesus had a public ministry of about three years. Up to then he
had lived a fairly ordinary life, as far as we can tell, for there is little record of his life apart from his birth and his visit to Jerusalem

when he was twelve. We know that he was obedient to his parents, as in Luke's Gospel we are told, 'Jesus increased in wisdom and in years, and in divine and human favour' (Luke 2:52). He worked with his hands, following Joseph's trade as a carpenter, and then, at the age of thirty, when most men would have been married and settled down with a family, he began his ministry. A sort of itinerant rabbi, a teacher, preacher and healer, accompanied by a group of twelve men, his disciples—'learners', pupils. An oddly assorted bunch, mostly ordinary working men, and if you had asked them why they had given up their homes and work to follow Jesus they would probably just have said, 'He called me', 'I wanted to know more' or 'I knew he was for me.' Where it was all leading they hadn't much clue, even though Jesus spent so much time with them explaining what he was about, and of God's kingdom, and the future one day they would enjoy. Lately, though, he had talked a lot about suffering and death, that he would be leaving them, then coming back for them, and it was all part of God's plan. They found that very difficult. In fact many people who had started out as followers had dropped out, gone back home, couldn't take it, especially when he spoke about eating his flesh and drinking his blood. This was altogether too much for some. 'This teaching is difficult—who can accept it?' they said as they turned away from him. Sometimes it was marvellous—the crowds flocking around, miracles being performed—and he was such a powerful speaker and teacher. It looked at times as though he was destined to lead the people to freedom from the Roman oppression. But then people were so fickle, and troublemakers stirred the crowds up against him, and the religious leaders wanted to get rid of him—he was an embarrassment to them. There were ominous signs of trouble ahead, and Jesus seemed to be heading straight into it. They knew him, and yet they didn't. Sometimes they understood everything he told them; at other times they could not make head or tail of it, and even when he told them over and over again they found it hard to take in. Or was it that they did not *want* to take in what he was telling them? Yet they knew he was different, he was special, he was... who was he really?

It was not only the disciples who asked themselves that question. Everybody was talking about him, passing their judgment. To those who had heard him, felt his touch, been healed or helped, he was wonderful, god-like, but others had no time for that. They knew him, where he came from: Nazareth. Nothing good came out of there, and anyway, he was only Joseph's son, that carpenter from Nazareth. But others said, 'Remember all that talk about his birth, and whether or not he was Joseph's son? Those were strange goings-on.' Not your ordinary sort of teacher, preacher, healer, was he? He was more like one of the old prophets come back, or even like that John the Baptist, or maybe it was Jeremiah... who knows?

So Jesus asked his disciples who people were saying he was. They were eager to tell him the various theories they had heard. A prophet for sure, a holy man, a man from God—oh yes, many people had been very complimentary, for a prophet was the highest category, more important than a priest or rabbi, teacher or healer.

Then comes the razor-sharp question: 'But who do *you* say that I am?' Here is the 'finals' question. I can imagine there was a stunned silence. Their jaws dropped, but no sound came, until Peter blurted out, 'You are the Messiah, the Son of the Living God.' He probably amazed himself—it just came out, all the feelings and emotions, the experiences of the past three years. With that direct question Peter is challenged to say what he believes, what he knows deep within himself. Commended by Jesus as the rock on which he will build the Church, Peter must have felt elated, proud, excited, confident. Now nothing would stop Jesus winning through, and Peter would be right there beside him. But within a very short while Jesus calls Peter a stumbling-block, for trying to divert him from following his calling to suffer and to die. Peter could not comprehend a suffering Messiah, or the Son of the living God actually dying. In spite of promising to stand by his Master, whatever happened, Peter failed and failed miserably, denying he had even met Jesus, and running away as Jesus was put to death. Yet Peter would know the joy of meeting his risen Lord, of being recommissioned as the rock Jesus said he would be, given the privilege of caring for the flock.

It is very easy for us, like the disciples, to answer the question, 'Who do people say that the Son of Man is?' We have heard it all! But what about the direct and searching question Jesus puts to us personally, as he did to them? 'But who do *you* say that I am?' I find that many people who would call themselves Christians, who belong to a church, are content to answer the first question, but not the second. I remember asking the question of a prominent church member at a Lent course. He glared at me and said, 'That is a matter between God and me!'—and I sensed an unease in the group in case I asked the question again. Yet we cannot avoid the question. We have to answer, and surely at the very least it will make us think deeply about our faith.

As I look at Jesus, the Jesus of history, the Jesus I see through the gospel accounts, I can say with Peter, 'You are the Messiah, the Son of the living God.' I have no doubt about that, but I can also say, as Thomas did, on meeting the risen Lord, 'My Lord and my God!' I can put a time and place on that first encounter, when I was converted, 'turned round', stepped out in faith acknowledging Jesus as my Saviour and my Lord—but it is a living relationship. Day by day, Jesus is my Lord and my God, and so many other things too. Each day I go on realizing that, experiencing it, and trying to share it with others. In spite of that, I, like Peter, fail to live up to my testimony over and over again, but I know where to go to for help, for forgiveness and renewal—to my Lord and my God. The young graduate with his degree still has a lot to learn. The degree was for starters. Now he has to build on what he knows by experience, and he will get it wrong many times before he arrives at a point when it all makes sense, and all works out.

The disciples had three years with Jesus; then they graduated, with varying degrees, and went on to live out, work out, their knowledge of him and their faith in him. To teach others, show others, introduce others to their Master. Two thousand years of Christian witness have gone by, and now here we stand on the edge of the third millennium. No wonder Jesus has been described as 'the Man who chopped history in half'. Frank Pagden in his book of that title says this:

> As we grow older we realize that the best gift we can wish for others is not to hear the most eloquent sermon, or be won over by the most attractive personality, but that in the middle of an ordinary day and ordinary concerns they may catch a glimpse of the grace of eternal love, and they may feel the touch of the finger of Christ, and recognize whose it is... the fascinating character who took a divine cleaver to human history and divided BC from AD'.

As we feel 'the touch of the finger of Christ' on our lives, let us be bold enough to respond to him, to tell him what he means to us, and to tell others too, so that they may begin on their journey. They can be encouraged, challenged and drawn to discover more of the one who is 'the Messiah, the Son of the living God' and make their own personal commitment to him.

Jesus, my shepherd, brother, friend,
my prophet, priest and King,
my Lord, my life, my way, my end,
accept the praise I bring.

Weak is the effort of my heart,
and cold my warmest thought,
but when I see thee as thou art,
I'll praise thee as I ought.

Till then I would thy love proclaim
with every fleeting breath,
and may the music of thy name
refresh my soul in death.

John Newton, 1725–1807

CHAPTER 15

Get switched on!

ISAIAH 60:1

Arise, shine; for your light has come, and the glory of the Lord has risen upon you.

My daughter Alison looked with horror at the pair of shoes in my hands. 'I hope, Mother, you are not thinking of wearing those today?' I informed her that I had every intention of wearing them for the very special occasion to which I had been invited. 'But you can't,' she protested. 'They are all different colours. They don't go with anything.' I sat down, put the shoes on and, stretching out my feet, announced, 'I know they are all different colours—that means they will go with anything!' I did wear them, and do wear them; and yes, they are bright, they are several colours, I like them and what is more, they are extremely comfortable!

Alison certainly got the message, for on my birthday just a couple of weeks later she gave me an illustrated copy of the poem entitled 'Warning. When I am an old woman I shall wear purple'. Jenny Joseph's wonderful poem is about a woman's intentions to 'live it up' when she gets old, and to do all the things she had wanted to do all her life, but had never dared. For me, though, I have always been prone to enjoying life to the full, and taking risks, without worrying too much about the consequences. I know too that my family understand that, and although they may feebly protest now and again, they do so with good humour and understanding. 'Be your age,' I was told some years ago, when I had launched out on some rather daring adventure, more suited to an active teenager than 'a lady of the cloth'. I remember answering, 'I shall never grow up, or act my age. Life is too short.' For what is age, what are the years? It is life that matters, and the living. I feel a great sense of affinity with the characters in the television series *Last of the Summer Wine* who find they can be boys again in old age, and enjoy doing the things they have always wanted to do, but were never allowed. In the series we see the marked contrast between those who are hemmed in by convention, by the dictates of others, and the three 'old boys' who are enjoying being themselves.

Jesus said we are to let our light shine, reflect the God-given light we have received, not hide it away under a tub. Why is it, I wonder, that we so often think we should be bland, restrained, even (dare I say it) dull? Maybe it is something that was instilled in us when we were young, when life for some of us was very much more sedate than it is today—a black and white world, with only a few shades of grey. Yet it is not only older people who are fearful of standing out. So many young people are content to be clones of each other, conforming to the uniform nature and expression of those around, 'fitting in'. Paul urged his fellow Christians, 'Do not be conformed to this world, but be transformed by the renewing of your minds, so that you may discern what is the will of God— what is good and acceptable and perfect' (Romans 12:2). We are not to be men and women in grey suits—that expression of conformity—but alive with light and colour. That message comes like a trumpet call through scripture, challenging us to be different: 'Arise, shine!'

The verse from Isaiah, 'Arise, shine; for your light has come, and the glory of the Lord has risen upon you', was pointed out to me not long after I had become a Christian. I was trying desperately to conform to what I thought a Christian young lady should be— restrained, quiet, 'proper'—and this verse was given to me to remind me that God had called me as me, and he wanted me to be freed to be myself, the me enlightened by the light of his glory, his son.

I remember interviewing a young Church Army Officer on Yorkshire Television some years ago and asking her what difference it had made to her life when she became a Christian. She said, 'That moment the sun shone brighter, the sky was bluer, the grass was greener and the birds sang sweeter.' What a marvellous description of the light of Christ coming into a life, and I can echo her experience, knowing the difference the light makes in the way I see life, the world, society and myself. I see the effect the light has on so many lives, young and old. I see the light shining through those who have experienced great tragedies in their lives, who have gone through dreadful suffering and loss. I see the light shining through those who are young and adventurous, who are on fire for God, wholeheartedly giving themselves in his service, and in people quietly getting on with life, sharing with their neighbours and friends the light of Christ. I see it in the lives of those who hold high office, and who stand out by their example of commitment and dedication to serve the community in which God has put them. I see it in the colourful characters who are not afraid to stand up and be counted. I see it in the faces of those who are on the point of passing from this world to the next. They are all very different people and situations, but the same light shines through.

It was dull and cloudy as I went into church early last Sunday to prepare for the service. I thought how cold it seemed in church, even though the heating had come on. How drab it looked, not very inviting at all. But as I came out of the vestry a few minutes later it was like looking through a kaleidoscope—the whole place was ablaze with dancing colours. The sun had come out and was shining through the stained-glass windows, transforming the whole place. I noticed the colours of the flowers, how bright the banners were on the pillars, and the floor and walls lit up with warmth and light. It seemed totally different from a few minutes previously. It even felt different, light and airy, and I felt different too, as though a burden had been lifted from my shoulders. Then the door opened, and I heard voices, and then in they came. Children, mums and dads, older people, folk on their own, others together. The sound of activity, books being got out, teacups tinkling ready for after the service. Cheerful chatter, everyone coming into the light, the warmth and dancing colour. As I went to greet people I looked into faces alight with the sheer joy of being there, being in church, with each other, coming to worship, to praise, to give thanks for 'the light of life'. John breezed up to me, 'Morning, Margaret. It looks like the sun's coming out this morning.' I looked around at the scene before me. 'It certainly does—makes all the difference, doesn't it?' I replied. And I didn't just mean the sunshine, either!

Colours of day dawn into the mind,
the sun has come up, the night is behind,
go down in the city, into the street,
and let's give the message to the people we meet.

So light up the fire, and let the flame burn,
open the door, let Jesus return.
Take seeds of his spirit, let the fruit grow,
tell the people of Jesus, let his love show.

Sue McClellan/Keith Rycroft/John Paculabo

CHAPTER 16

Insurance or assurance?

MATTHEW 6:19–21

*Do not store up for yourselves treasures on earth,
where moth and rust consume and where thieves break in and
steal; but store up for yourselves treasures in heaven,
where neither moth nor rust consumes and where thieves do not
break in and steal. For where your treasure is, there your
heart will be also.*

Children do not think about them, young people have no time
for them, old people relinquish them, those treasures on earth.
That is a generalization, of course, but most children soon tire of
those expensive gifts which loving parents and, more often, grand-
parents go to endless trouble to provide for them. Just before each
Christmas, there seems to be one special toy 'everybody' wants,
and which cannot be got for love or money. We are told that unless
that toy is produced on Christmas morning, then Christmas will be
ruined, not just for the child, but for the whole family. The search
for this item seems to become a matter of life and death, and we
are given constant updates as to the possible sources. On the news
we see scenes of near riot as people fight over those precious
things, and a flushed but victorious purchaser is seen clutching
one, as though it was the World Cup. I can tell you, as someone
who in years past has gone through all this, that come the week
after Christmas, or even sooner, that toy will have lost its appeal,
and will be found discarded under the bed, or at the back of a cupboard. Children are like that, and thank goodness they are! Things
lose their appeal and charm, are soon discarded for other more
interesting things, like the boxes and packaging those treasures
came in!

Young people, late teens and twenties, tend to 'travel light'.
Their aim is to be with friends, see the world, be part of the throw-
away society. Cash is for spending, not saving, possessions are for
the moment, not for storing, people have a 'use it or bin it' attitude. Parents despair that their offspring take life too lightly, and
grumble, 'Why doesn't he settle down, think about the future?' I

admire and applaud the young people who do take a year out, backpack around the world, or spend time working as volunteers either at home or overseas, and one of my great delights is to meet the many young people from all over the world who come to be part of the Christian community at Scargill House in the Dales, for a year or so. Working in the house and on the estate, caring for the guests who come for holidays or to attend a conference, so as to learn what living in a Christian community is all about, and to find their purpose in life. On their allowances they cannot afford to build up a bank balance, but they certainly will learn about the treasures of heaven!

As people grow older they often discover that those things they have held on to have lost their appeal, become outdated, and yes, the moths and the rust have taken their toll! With the accumulation of things over the years they now feel 'cluttered up' and so begin to get rid of things. For many people it is a case of having to get rid of them, through having to move to smaller accommodation or go into care, or because they just don't have the time or energy to look after those things. Cherished sporting equipment gathers dust when the owner can no longer use it, precious ornaments get knocked over and chipped beyond repair because the hand that holds the duster is shaky, and eyes can no longer guide the hand. Money in the bank, those stocks and shares, put away 'for a rainy day' have not proved to be the pleasure they were intended to be, for now it seems too late to enjoy them. How often I am told by elderly people, 'We always meant to spend it on a cruise, go on a long holiday, but now it's too late… If only…' So why do we do it, becoming so concerned about things, and when do we start on this path? I have come to think it is a disease of middle age which, if not dealt with, can prove fatal. Maybe it starts through a 'keeping up with the Joneses' mentality, wanting to have a bigger extension, more expensive car, more elaborate furnishings. It can arise through getting hooked on collections of this, that or the other, 'because they will increase in value'. There is also the fear and uncertainty about the future generated so often by the advertisements of investment companies, banks and finance houses, and the worry that should illness strike, or old age arrive, then we would not be able to manage.

Of course it is good to enjoy our homes and leisure, it is right to be sensible about providing for the future, but when it becomes the be-all and end-all of everything, we get life out of perspective. I can think of a man who delighted in his small collection of antiques, and loved to show them off. He visited sale rooms and antique fairs and gradually built up a large collection, but it began to become an obsession. He could think of little else. He worried his home might be broken into and his antiques stolen, so he went to great trouble and expense to have all the latest alarms fitted. Then he decided his antiques would be better out of sight, so he stored them in his loft. He became so anxious that he stopped going on holiday or visiting, in case someone, knowing he was away, broke in. What had begun as a pleasurable hobby became a terrible burden. The enjoyment had gone and all he had left was worry.

Another man, a brilliant businessman, had such fun building up his first business, and then added another, and another, and another... working all hours, flying all over the world, spending time in this conference and that meeting. It so took over his life that his marriage broke up, he drifted away from the church and his friends, and from all accounts is still on the same path. He is a millionaire, but at what cost?

Children and young people are too busy enjoying each day to think about storing up treasures for their own sakes; the very old often regret they spent so much of their lives accumulating things that they failed to appreciate the ordinary everyday gifts of life. 'If only I had my time over again, I wouldn't make the same mistake,' they say sadly, for they know, as we all know, that we do not get our time again. This life is the real thing, and not a dummy run.

Sadly, the middle-aged often dismiss the memories of childhood and youth, and have not learned the value of listening to the warnings of the old. Whatever age we are, we are never too young or too old to benefit from the words of Jesus, and find release from the burdens, which we may have thought were treasures!

Enjoy what you have, share what you have, sit light to what you have. That way you will live happily, generously, hopefully. That is the message that comes to me through reading the Sermon on the Mount, and particularly through the warnings about possessiveness. I am so often tempted to hoard, to say, 'That is mine', to build up my own little pile. Then I hear Jesus saying, 'Where your treasure is, there your heart will be also' and I have to think, 'Where is my heart, what really matters?'

I see too, all around me, so many shining examples of people who have discovered the genuine treasures of heaven rather than settling for earthly counterfeits. Like those young people at Scargill House, enjoying life to the full even when they are getting up at crack of dawn to pray together before cleaning the toilets, washing the floors and making sure the meals are prepared for the guests. Then they still respond with a smile to all those guests who keep asking, 'How long have you been here, where did you come from, when will you be getting a proper job?' I see it in the vicar of a parish in the north-east who tells me, 'We have cracked the problems of break-ins, we don't get them now' and goes on to say, 'Well, they've pinched everything we had of value, so they don't bother now. We have enough to get by. They probably feel sorry for us, their stuff's better than ours!' Then he laughs and says, 'But it's a great life, Margaret. I wouldn't change it for the world!' and I know he means it.

I see it in the old lady, now confined to a small room in a residential home, who tells me, 'I thank God every day for what he's given me. I've had a wonderful life, and now I haven't a worry in the world. They are all so kind to me here...' As I look at all those youngsters at church giving up their time to wash cars to raise money for famine relief, in the sound of laughter in the church hall kitchen where a band of willing cooks are slaving over hot stoves preparing a meal for us to enjoy. I see it in a group buckling down to Bible study, even though it is very new to them all, and the excitement on their faces as they discover treasures within those pages. I see it when I come across a couple of friends quietly praying together—both of them are going through a hard patch, and yet their concern is for others. They tell me, 'We know how much prayer helps us, so we thought we'd just get together and pray for those in hospital.' Every day I discover new treasures, and I could not put a price on them—they are beyond price. I find the treasures in the strangest places and in unexpected situations, but they are 'more precious than gold' and, as an old expression puts it, 'worth more than all the tea in China!'

We could live in a mansion, have the latest in modern technology, possess the finest antiques, the biggest bank balance, and have an army at our command, but how do they compare with the treasures that God gives us every day, if only we recognize them? What are they, compared with the riches we have in Christ? How do they rate beside the gifts of the Spirit?

I have just been re-reading a Media Relations report on the Hillsborough tragedy that happened on Saturday 15 April 1989. It was written by Roy Arnold, a parish priest and also the communications officer for the Diocese of Sheffield. As one of those early on the scene, he speaks of what it was like to be part of the horror and tragedy of that event, and how it has affected him, looking back on it all. He finishes his very moving report with these words: 'I am bashing this out on an old-style manual typewriter, the kind I feel most comfortable with. I have not got a Filofax, nor an electronic diary, nor a portable fax machine. They might all have been useful on the night. However, I do always carry with me that most portable of prayers, the Jesus prayer—"Lord Jesus Christ, Son of God, have mercy on us."' That is what I call treasure, and treasure that lasts for ever. I thank God for Roy, and all those others who have shown me the reality of the words of Jesus, and the treasure we can have by living life in the light of those words.

What do superfluous riches profit in this world, when you find in
them neither a succour in birth nor a defence against death? For
without a covering are we born into the world, with our provision
we depart hence, and in the grave we have no inheritance.

Ambrose, c. 339–97

Plenteous grace with thee is found,
grace to cover all my sin.
Let the healing streams abound,
make and keep me pure within.
Thou of life the fountain art,
freely let me take of thee.
Spring thou up within my heart,
rise to all eternity.

Charles Wesley, 1707–1788

CHAPTER 17

Known by name

ISAIAH 43:1b & 4a

*Do not fear, for I have redeemed you; I have called you
by name, you are mine … Because you are precious in my sight,
and honoured, and I love you.*

Those personalized invitations drop through our letterboxes giving news of amazing and unrepeatable offers—at a price. 'You have been specially selected…'. One arrived on my birthday this year, congratulating me on the occasion, and suggesting it was time I made provision for the future! It is not difficult to see through these so-called 'personal' invitations. Our particulars have been taken from a list, gleaned through past purchases, or from our responding to survey forms we filled in, which promised us exciting free gifts. Many and varied are the ways of market research, and they know that we consumers are more likely to read something addressed to us personally than to a circular mailshot. Equally, the phone call, usually at tea-time, and a friendly voice which says, 'Good evening, Mrs Cundiff, I am just ringing to let you know we have our representative in your area tonight…' They may have our name and use it, but personal it is not! How different the letter from a friend, a phone call—whatever the time—from a loved one, the cheery greeting of a neighbour, and the excitement of finding a message 'Be with you soon, love…' The personal touch is so important, but it has to be the real thing, not a commercial imitation.

The Bible is the Word of God. It is God speaking not only to his people at a particular time for a particular situation, but for all people, all time. He uses many messengers and many means of getting his word through to us, but because it is his living word then it is personal, addressed to us, intended for us, so that we might know and enjoy that special personal relationship with him. The wonder of the Bible is that we can read a sentence, a verse, a passage many times, understand its context, grasp its meaning, but then there are times when it comes alive in such a personal way that we know it is for us at that very moment. Whether it is as we read and meditate on our own or in a group, or listen to it read aloud, it comes bearing a clear personal message. There is communication at the deepest level, if we will hear and receive it. In the Anglican tradition the lessons read publicly end with the reader saying, 'This is the Word of the Lord,' with the response, 'Thanks be to God.' I feel that maybe we would take notice and listen more attentively if those words came at the beginning of the readings, not the end! I find that phrase, 'This is the Word of the Lord' quite awesome. The message is that God is speaking to me, now; he wants me to receive it and be thankful for it, not just unthinkingly respond parrot-fashion.

Although I had read the 43rd chapter of Isaiah many times, had studied the background of it, enjoyed the poetic flow of the words, it was not until it touched me with blinding clarity personally that I realized that here was the message to help me see my life in a new light—God's word *to me*. It was a time when I was searching for my own identity, trying to discover the real me. I was many things: a daughter, wife, mother. A deaconess, broadcaster, television advisor, friend, neighbour, colleague, holding various titles and positions— but who was the real person, what was her purpose? As a mere speck of humanity confined to a short space of time, how could I relate to God's divine plan? How dare I even think I might make any difference in this world at all, this insignificant grain of sand pushed around by the tides of life, a seed blown by the wind aimlessly here and there? Then God spoke! 'Do not fear, for I have redeemed you; I have called you by name, you are mine.' Don't be frightened, you belong to me, I know you personally, by name, *you*. That was the word of release and freedom, enabling me to realize that I did not need to put on an act, pretend, try and make a good impression. Neither could I think that I could get away with anything, as if God neither knew nor cared. He knew my name, knew me, understood me, and would be always there for me. Precious, honoured, loved, a daughter of the King! That was and will always be my status—what more do I need? He knows my name, knows me.

Constantly I meet people who feel that they are useless, of no value to anyone or anything. This feeling is compounded by modern society where we are so easily reduced to a PIN number, a digit on a computer printout, a nameless item, part of a vast army providing statistics, graphs, social groupings, judged by the pieces of plastic we hold and use, and our 'consumer spending power'. Tough if we are at the bottom end of the market, frightening as we contemplate the numbers game, and our place in it. To dehumanize a person, to give them just a number—there's nothing new in that. Slaves were branded with a number, as were prisoners in wartime concentration camps. Today it seems we are eager to become numbers, to receive in return for our name that little piece of plastic, which is supposed to be the answer to all our needs. But the big questions of life are still, 'Where did I come from, why am I here, where am I going?' and the biggest question is surely, 'But who am I?' And God reaches out to us: 'Do not fear!' He knows us as people, and whatever we may think of ourselves, and whatever others may think, he says we are precious, gives us a place of honour, and loves us. When we recognize this, it can make all the difference to how we see ourselves, and how we should see others too. They also are known by name, they too are precious, honoured and loved.

Archbishop Desmond Tutu, the much loved and respected former Archbishop of Cape Town, is still one of the most celebrated and influential men in the world of today. When he was a boy of twelve, growing up in South Africa, he had a life-changing experience. His mother was sweeping a verandah when the then Father Trevor Huddleston, a missionary monk, walked by. Father Huddleston stopped, took off his hat and greeted Desmond's mother. Archbishop Tutu says, 'I had never seen anyone do this to a black woman, let alone an uneducated woman like my mother. It was a great influence on me.' It was a simple act of acknowledging another person as equally precious, regardless of race, sex, colour or position; affording her honour, as a sister, a member of the same family—God's family. God spoke to Desmond through that act of courtesy to his mother, and he discovered his own worth too. And through his life and ministry countless others have been enabled to do the same, of all races, cultures and backgrounds. Archbishop Trevor Huddleston, as he became, is now dead, but his witness lives on, not least through that simple act of stopping to raise his hat to a black woman, in recognition of their God-given relationship.

When Jesus rose from the dead, he made it known first not by a fanfare of trumpets, a dramatic public announcement, a sensational visitation to the leaders of the city or even to the assembled group of frightened followers hiding behind closed doors. He spoke to a woman who stood weeping by his empty tomb, calling her by name, 'Mary'. In that meeting Mary knew she was precious, honoured, loved, and entrusted with the greatest news of all time, a personal message, as it still is for each one of us. 'Do not fear, I have redeemed you, I have called you by name...' It is the word of the Lord through the prophet Isaiah, revealed in Jesus, the living Word, the redeemer of all mankind. Jesus calls us by name, invites us to share with him his new life here and now and for all eternity.

God gave everything for us: he gave his son to die for us, to live in us, and his Holy Spirit to enable us to understand, enjoy, and share our inheritance. The promise is for all time to all generations, and each individual. 'Do not fear, for I am with you; I will bring your offspring from the east, and from the west I will gather you; I will say to the north, "Give them up," and to the south, "Do not withhold"; bring my sons from far away, and my daughters from the end of the earth—everyone who is called by my name, whom I created for my glory, whom I formed and made' (Isaiah 43:5–7).

Say to yourself, 'I am loved by God more than I can either conceive or understand.' Let this fill all your soul and all your prayers and never leave you. You will soon see that this is the way to find God.

Henri De Tourville, *Letters of Direction*

CHAPTER 18

Forgiveness
— fact or fiction?

1 JOHN 1:8–9

If we say that we have no sin, we deceive ourselves, and the truth is not in us. If we confess our sins, he who is faithful and just will forgive us our sins and cleanse us from all unrighteousness.

Some words in the newspaper article caught my eye: 'A lie is always a betrayal—a betrayal of the truth.' It was a comment on a real-life situation, but I was thinking about the publicity that was surrounding a fictional character, Deirdre Rachid of *Coronation Street*, the long-running popular series on television. In the story-line Deirdre had been duped by her fiancé, Jon, into taking part in a mortgage fraud, and had been jailed for it. He had spun a web of deceit, pretending to be a single pilot, when he was a married salesman, and poor Deirdre was left deserted and deceived, and paying the price. It had aroused such public outrage that even the Prime Minister and Leader of the Opposition were drawn into the argument, and campaigns launched for Deirdre's release. Pictures of a tearful Deirdre behind bars made every newspaper, and even editorials were devoted to her situation, a strange case of confusion between fact and fiction in so many minds.

What it did show was that betrayal of one person by another, whether in fact or in fiction, touches the emotions to a powerful extent. There is a sense of outrage kindled by sympathy for the deceived victim. When someone is betrayed by a lover, colleague, relative or friend, it seems an even greater offence than betrayal by a stranger, casual acquaintance or enemy. This is so poignantly expressed in Psalm 41: 'Even my bosom friend in whom I trusted, who ate of my bread, has lifted the heel against me' (v. 9). In those few words the grief and sadness are so evident, the despair over a relationship that went sour. Life is strewn with stories of betrayal, and they are to be found as much in the pages of scripture as in today's newspaper. Perhaps one of the most tragic accounts of betrayal in the Old Testament is that of Samson by Delilah, and we have the picture of the great man Samson reduced to a blinded and bound figure of fun through his betrayal by the woman he loved and trusted.

Yet when we think about betrayal there is one name that is forever linked to it—that of Judas. Judas had been chosen, called to be a friend of Jesus, one of the Twelve. The one the others trusted too, for he was the one who looked after the money, the treasurer. We know very little about him, but his concern for money was evident in his response to Mary anointing the feet of Jesus with the costly perfume. He saw it as a waste, something that could have been converted into hard cash rather than given as a love offering, fragrantly evaporating into thin air. It was a short step from that to 'coming to a business arrangement' to betray Jesus for money, the thirty pieces of silver, the value he put on the one who had given him love, trust, dignity, and authority. Jesus knew what had happened, yet still gave him the chance to change. It is hard to comprehend how Judas could have allowed Jesus to wash his feet, to receive from his Lord's hand the bread and wine—the great symbols of oneness, trust, fellowship and love—and still do what he did; and the ultimate betrayal was surely in sealing it with a kiss. Had he ever truly loved Jesus, or had he become disappointed in the way things had worked out? Was he a cold, calculating money-grabber, or caught up in something that carried him along so fast that he could not withdraw? What we do know is that when it dawned on him just what he had done, he wanted to put the clock back. He acknowledged he had sinned, that he had betrayed an innocent man, but there was no way out. And so in his despair, his guilt, he hanged himself. He could not face up to being the instrument of his Master's death.

Our natural response to Judas, the betrayer, is to condemn him, despise him, even applaud his downfall. Sometimes this frightens me, for I am aware that in all of us there is the seed of betrayal. Which one of us can put our hand on our heart and say we have never betrayed anyone, have never in our lives betrayed the truth by telling a lie, distorted the truth, and so caused suffering to another, even to someone who trusted us, loved us? How many times have I wished I could put the clock back, take back a word, thought or action which has injured another person, whether intentionally or not, whatever the motive. When I think of Judas I see a tragic figure who took a wrong turning. For when he came to his senses, and I am sure that he did, he turned in the wrong direction. He went to those who compounded his sin, instead of turning to the one who would have forgiven him, restored him. The clock could not have been put back; Jesus would still have gone to the cross, Judas or no Judas. But Judas could have known the cleansing, loving, restoring touch that Jesus offered to all who turned to him and still offers freely to us today, whatever our situation. We may find it hard to forgive, we so easily pass judgment on our fellow men and women and set our 'cut-off' points. We need to ask ourselves some very searching questions, and be honest about our own attitudes and our predetermined conclusions.

Do we limit the power of forgiveness? Do we limit the love of Jesus? Think of the thief on the cross, who could only incline his head towards Jesus and whisper, 'Remember me.' Think of Peter, who swore he did not know, had never even met Jesus. What of those who ran away and deserted Jesus in his time of need, those who slept when he had asked them to stay awake with him? Was there forgiveness for them? As we look at our own lives, as we face up to the truth about ourselves—whether in the cold light of day, or as we contemplate in a time of confession alone or in the company of others—how can we be sure we have not gone beyond the bounds of forgiveness? The answer comes from Jesus himself, 'For God so loved the world that he gave his only Son, so that everyone who believes in him may not perish but may have eternal life' (John 3:16). That world includes Judas, Peter, you and me. All that is asked is that we repent, turn from ourselves to Jesus, accept his word of forgiveness, live it out in our lives, and share it with others.

The tragedy for so many people is that they feel they are beyond the pale, beyond God's love, beyond forgiveness and a new life. Only this week a man came to me in tears, saying, 'I can't expect God to forgive me, I'm too far gone now.' When I asked him who told him that, he just looked at me and said, 'Well, that's how I feel about it.' But he had made the first step in the right direction by sharing with someone else how he felt, and we were able together to begin to explore what God's word said, what Jesus had done, and what he promised to anyone who would turn to him. 'It's not what you expect, but what God says that matters,' I

assured him. He looked at me, and then said, 'How do you know?'
I replied, 'Because he has done it for me, and you are no different.'

Where God's love and mercy are concerned, we are all the same.
The difference is how we see ourselves, and how we see and treat
others.

> *If we are sinners forgiven, we ought to behave as forgiven, wel-*
> *comed home, crowned with wonderful love in Christ, and so cheer*
> *and encourage all about us, who often go heavily because we*
> *reflect our gloom upon them instead of our grateful love, hope,*
> *confidence.*

Those words by Father Congreve in his *Spiritual Letters* speak
volumes to me as I go about my daily life, as I try to come to terms
with the world around me and within me, and as I, by the grace of
God, enjoy the new life he has given me, and that he goes on
renewing day by day.

> *God forgives you,*
> *Forgive others,*
> *Forgive yourself.*

> *Through Christ, God has put away your sin,*
> *Approach your God in peace.*

A New Zealand Prayer Book

CHAPTER 19

God's agenda

MICAH 6:8

*He has told you, O mortal, what is good; and what does
the Lord require of you but to do justice, and to love kindness,
and to walk humbly with your God?*

When Jesus was brought before Pilate for sentence, Pilate found himself faced with a terrible dilemma. He recognized that Jesus was innocent of the charge against him, but he was afraid of those who were violently opposed to Jesus, for he could see that there might be violent repercussions if they were thwarted in their demands for his execution. Pilate wanted peace at any price; he valued his own career and well-being above the life of the one who was causing such a stir. It would be easier and politically expedient to give in to the Jewish leaders—after all, it was their affair, not his.

As Jesus calmly stands before him and challenges Pilate with, 'Everyone who belongs to the truth hears my voice' (John 18:37), Pilate can only reply, 'What is truth?' Does the truth really matter in such a situation, when expediency would solve his problem? The truth stood there before him, and Pilate had no excuses, but he could not face up to the implications of hearing the truth and following it. And so the greatest miscarriage of justice stands in his name. Jesus 'was crucified under Pontius Pilate'. Pilate may have washed his hands as an expression of denying responsibility for the death of Jesus, but all the hand-washing and hand-wringing in the world could not absolve him of his guilt. Pilate is not unique, though. We see the same sort of situation happening throughout history, and in our world today. There are those occasions when outside influences and threats, coupled with internal fears and conflicts, lead to biased judgments, the scales blatantly tipped one way or the other. So often, things are whitewashed to make them look presentable.

The prophet Micah recognized this trait in the life of his society—the injustices, the rotten root, the exploitations of the people. He speaks of scant measure, wicked scales, dishonest weights, violence, lies, tongues of deceit (Micah 6:10–12). He sees so-called justice clothed in the trappings of empty ritual, people merely going through the motions with no intention of seeing that right was done. Micah thunders out the warning that it is no use coming with sacrifices, bowing low before God, when people are practising such wickedness. It is not enough to pay lip-service to justice—it has to be honestly and openly carried out. Judgment must be based on the evidence and not on influence and emotion.

In the words of Lord Hewart, 'A long line of cases shows that it is not merely of some importance, but it is of fundamental importance, that justice should not only be done, but should manifestly and undoubtedly be seen to be done.' A clear statement of the standard expected. As a judge said recently, sentencing a man who was a well-known figure, 'You must understand that I sentence you for what you did, not who you are.' He had weighed the evidence before him and made his judgment purely on that, and rightly so. May we always be able to enjoy that standard in our courts. But it is not enough for us to approve of justice, to admire those who are professionally engaged in pursuing it. We are all required by God 'to do justice', and that means in the judgments we pass on others, the influences we bring to bear, our own dealings with others, and our participation in the life of society in our world.

As we come to the new millennium, more and more people are catching the vision through Jubilee 2000 and similar organizations to work for justice for people of the Third World who are crippled by debt. Demonstrations, petitions, constant lobbying of world and national leaders, have begun to have some effect, raising the profile of the world debt issue, but there are also many other issues which call for our attention and action right here and now. We need to heed the single plaintive cry for justice, as well as that of the many screaming to be heard, who hit the headlines so dramatically. Justice is an everyday issue—are we doing it? We have a voice, we have a pocket and we can pray—we have no excuse for failing to do justice, have we?

But there is far more to it than this. We are also called upon 'to love kindness', to 'hate the sin, but love the sinner'. But so often we cannot distinguish between the two, and what about the sinned against? Do they receive the kindness they need? Often they are forgotten. Our son shakes his head when sometimes I go on about what I think are harsh sentences passed down by the courts, for he is a Legal Officer, with almost twenty years' experience of working in the Magistrates Court, and knows the situation far better than I do. He tells me, 'You talk about being kind and understanding, of shorter sentences, overlooking what they have done, but what if it was Dad who had been mugged, Alison raped, Grandpa knocked down and killed by a drunken driver? What would you say then?' I get his point, and I honestly don't know how I would feel or act if I looked at the person who had done such a thing to one of my loved ones. There are shining examples of forgiveness seen even in such awful situations, but could I forgive? Where is the dividing point between justice and kindness? There must be justice or else society collapses; there has to be justice for the sake of both offender and the offended against, but then kindness can be shown, the recognition of a fellow human being. Like us, he or she is made in the image of God, but, also like us, they have marred and distorted that image. 'There but for the grace of God go I' is true for each one of us. Paul urges us, 'Be kind to one another, tender hearted, forgiving one another, as God in Christ has forgiven you' (Ephesians 4:32). It is personal, that call to us to show kindness, to forgive those who have hurt us. We cannot forgive on behalf of others, only for our own part, but it is the kindness that we have received that can influence the way we behave towards each other.

Kindness does not mean a weak sort of softness, or turning a blind eye to wrongdoing, but active concern and care for others, wanting the very best for them and doing our utmost to help them on their way, to make life easier and happier. What a difference even the smallest act of kindness makes! It can completely change a life, an intention, an action. We may leave ourselves wide open to ridicule, to being taken advantage of, but what has God in Christ done for us? Did we deserve his love, the sacrifice he made on the cross for us so we might live? If we only received justice we would be in a sorry state without any hope for the future.

Showing kindness ought to be a natural reaction in our everyday lives to other people. Simple acts like a helping hand, a smile, a minute or two of time given—these are such ordinary things, yet of immense value. There are so many examples that it is hard to include just one, but this week I went into a large department store at a very busy time to buy a small gift. Not sure where to find it in the store, I asked for help. The assistant smiled at me. 'I'll show you what we have,' she said, and took me over to the stand and explained the various items on display. Having chosen what I wanted I took it to the counter to pay for it. She commented, 'Did you say it was for a present? Would you like it gift-wrapped?' An unexpected act of kindness, but it made my day, and I hope made me a little kinder to those I met as I continued my shopping. It is a very simple example of kindness shown, but to me all part of that wider picture of God's plan for us, his requirement of us.

In Psalm 85 we have the vision of what our world could be like if only we lived by his plan. 'Surely his salvation is at hand for those who fear him, that his glory may dwell in our land. Steadfast love and faithfulness will meet; righteousness and peace will kiss each other. Faithfulness will spring up from the ground, and righteousness will look down from the sky' (Psalm 85:9–11).

The picture of God's glory dwelling in our world, our land, our community—what a perfect picture that is of God's kingdom here on earth. Is it possible? When there is justice and kindness shown, when we learn to walk humbly with our God, in faith, obedience, trust, then it is indeed possible. But it is up to us. The call comes to us.

In the New Revised Standard Version of the Bible, from which I have quoted, Micah 6:8 says, 'He has told you...' but I find the Revised Standard Version much more powerful, for it says, 'He has showed you, O man, what is good...' God has not just told us, but shown us what justice, kindness, forgiveness, truth and love are all about. He has shown us through Jesus. Here is our example, and here is also the means of our becoming what he wants us to be.

Are we willing, with true humility, to walk with him, learn from him? That is the question, that is the challenge. It is the way of joy and fulfilment, not just for ourselves but for those whose lives are touched by him through us. Is it asking too much of us? Look at Jesus, and then give your answer.

> *O God, who has so greatly loved us, long sought us,*
> *and mercifully redeemed us, give us grace that in everything we*
> *may yield ourselves, our wills and our works, a continual thank*
> *offering to you, through Jesus Christ our Lord.*

From the Westminster Confession of Faith 1647

CHAPTER 20

Go on and say it

PHILIPPIANS 1:3—4

*I thank my God every time I remember you, constantly praying
with joy in every one of my prayers for all of you.*

The young man had everything—or so I thought. First-class qual-
ifications, proven ability, a fine brain and impeccable background.
While I enthused about him, my companion looked pensive.
'Don't you agree?' I asked him. 'Oh yes, I agree with all you say,
but he has a very limited vocabulary, which could be a problem.'
I thought about that and frowned. I had found him to be very
eloquent, able to express himself perfectly, but my companion continued, 'He does not seem to know the words "please" or "thank
you".' Time alone will tell whether that young man will learn the
value of those words, but it certainly gave me a jolt, not just in relation to someone else, but to myself. Is my vocabulary limited in
that way? I confess that sometimes it is, when I am so busy thinking about what I am doing and where I am going that I fail to
notice other people. I end up accepting their unobtrusive kindness
and consideration without response. Yet I know how much a
'thank you' means to me—it can completely change my day, give
me the incentive to keep going, even when things might be difficult. It has a 'knock-on' effect too—it makes me want to respond
to others in like manner. It's a bit like throwing a pebble into a
pond, and seeing the ripples spread out.

Paul always begins his letters to the churches (with the notable
exception of that to the Galatians) with an expression of thanks for
them. The Galatians were causing him trouble, he did not feel
thankful for them, and he goes straight in at them to sort them
out—but all the other churches give him great joy, and he wants
them to know that. He gives thanks to God for them, and he tells
them so. Can you imagine how they felt to read that, to know that?

Those first-generation Christians had a tough time. Viewed with
suspicion, treated with contempt, subject to persecution and very
much on their own, just a tiny group amid other religions and
cultures. Young in faith and experience, subject to all sorts of

pressures, and without having easy access to their leaders, they still held fast to their faith, showing in their lives such love and enthusiasm, joy in fellowship and courage in difficulty that they grew rapidly in numbers. Paul longed to be able to visit them, be with them, teach and encourage them. But with the demands and distance and time in prison, Paul had to rely on getting letters through to them to instruct and encourage them, answering their questions, sorting out their problems, and not least warning them of those who would try to lure them away by claiming to have a superior gospel. There would be news too of what was happening with their fellow Christians in other places, and of Paul's own experiences where he was, with greetings from those who were with him, or who had visited him. His letters, of which we only have a few (there must have been many more written), would have been eagerly read, shared and kept safe so that what was contained could go on providing guidelines for faith and conduct, with the reminder that Paul was thanking God for them, praying for them, for they were so special to him. What an encouragement that must have been to them, and all those who read the letters!

Do we thank God for each other, I wonder? A former colleague of mine, David, would often gently rebuke me when I grumbled about a difficult person, or problems with a group, by saying, 'Margaret, they are God's gift to us!' And he was right, and I found that as I said thank you to God for them and prayed for them, then somehow my attitude changed towards them. They seemed much nicer, easier to get on with, or maybe it was I who had been changed. Whichever way it was, it worked. I also remember David adding, with a twinkle in his eyes, 'And remember, too, we are God's gift to them!' I find that taking this attitude to others makes all the difference, especially with someone with whom it is not always easy to get on. I need to see them as they are in God's eyes, and recognize their gifts rather than dwelling on their seeming failures; not only saying thank you for them, but *to* them. I have a number of very close and much loved friends with whom at one time I felt I would never be able to get on. God works miracles of grace in us and for us, and the words 'thank you' have a very important part to play in our recognizing that.

Each month I take a service of holy communion at a home for the elderly in our parish, and a group from our church comes along to help. Many of the residents are very frail, suffering from memory loss, and confused. Yet as they receive communion all of them respond by saying or mouthing, 'Thank you.' I think it is the most beautiful liturgical response I know. It may not be the Prayer Book response but it is the response that touches the heart of God—and those of us who are privileged to share with these dear saints. One old gentleman always used to respond, 'Thank you, darling,' and another by reaching out and squeezing my hand.

I have a lovely collection of letters and drawings from children of the various schools I visit. These 'thank you' letters contain wonderful illustrations of what they thought I had been talking to them about. I get so much enjoyment from them, and I thank God for their expressions of thanks, and the love they show so delightfully.

As I was leaving church the other Sunday morning, one of the children ran up to me to show me what she had been doing in Junior Church. It was a very bright painting of Abraham and Sarah beside their tent. She explained the story to me: 'Abraham and Sarah went on a long journey, and then Sarah had a baby boy.' I asked where the baby was. 'He's in the tent in his pram.' I agreed with her that he probably was, to keep him out of the sun. Then she looked up at me and said, 'Thank you, Mrs Cundiff.' 'What for?' I asked. 'Because you are you,' came her reply, and off she went. I have to admit to a big lump in my throat and a very warm feeling in my heart. 'Thank you' does that to us, doesn't it? And it is worth remembering too. But what about when the opposite happens, what effect does that have?

I have just been re-reading David Wilbourne's book *Archbishop's Diary* and in it he describes organizing a day for ordinands—those preparing for the ministry—at Bishopthorpe Palace. It went very well, and he speaks of being 'happily exhausted' at the end of it. He goes on to say, though, '...the Archbishop's sole comment was about the altar candles in chapel which had burnt out during the service. "You're getting meaner with those candles—you should have replaced them. It wasn't a good example to set."' David follows that up with another story. 'I recalled a church garden party which had gone with a swing. The sun had shone, the band had played, the stalls had sold out, profits broke all records. Everyone was delighted. Nearly everyone. One old man marched up to the vicar and pointed an accusing finger at him. "Now tell me, what would you have done if it had rained?" There's always one.' Perhaps, in the words of a well-known comedian, 'There's no answer to that!'—but it does show the shadow that can be cast over an otherwise happy event through the lack of voiced appreciation.

On a happier note, one evening in the autumn I went to conduct a Harvest Festival service in a little village chapel out in the country. It was a terrible night, and we all moaned and said what a rotten night it was, what a pity it was raining, and how it would keep folk from turning out. Then one man told me the story of an old local preacher who comes to that chapel on his bicycle. 'He always begins with a prayer saying thank you to God for the gift of the day. One night it was an even worse night than tonight, cold, windy, throwing it down with rain, and the old man arrived wet through. We thought he won't be able to start off in his usual way, thanking God for the day, not for this one. Then the old man got into the pulpit and began to pray. "Lord, we thank you for this day which you have given to us, and that we don't get many as bad as it…"' I said, 'I'll remember that one!' and going home that night I thanked God for the evening, for what we had enjoyed together, and for the story to remind me to say thank you, even in the direst circumstances—to be thankful that, unlike the old man who came by bike, I had the luxury of a car to get me home through the wind and rain. And to be grateful for the 'thank you' gift of flowers given to me, with love, for sharing with them in saying 'thank you' to God for the gift of the harvest. And to be thankful for the gift of worship, and for the gift of each other, and above all for the greatest gift of all, Jesus.

Father, you must get tired of our complaints, our demands and pleadings, the way we try to bend you to our will, sometimes shouting and hammering away at you, other times totally disregarding you. We turn our backs on you, telling you by the way we act that we think we can do very nicely without you, and anyway, it is all your fault when things go wrong—why don't you do something? I wouldn't blame you if you washed your hands of us, and left us to our own devices, because we are so ungrateful at times, so lacking in appreciation of you or of our fellow men and women.

Yet you love us, and have shown us your love in giving us
your Son, Jesus Christ and given us too the gift of one another to
share with, to learn from, to love as brothers and sisters.
So I just want to say thank you for being you, for always being at
hand, always loving and understanding me, providing for me.
Thank you for all those brothers and sisters you have given to me,
and thank you... for everything, for ever and ever. Amen.

CHAPTER 21

Have fun!

*This is the day that the Lord has made; let us rejoice
and be glad in it.*

This is a verse from one of the group of psalms sung to celebrate the Passover, and if you ever feel the need for a message of cheer, something to celebrate, a 'pick me up', turn to the 'Praise the Lord' psalms, from Psalm 111 to 118. I guarantee that before you get to the last verse, 'O give thanks to the Lord, for he is good, for his steadfast love endures for ever' (Psalm 118:29) you will feel a new person, you will have a spring in your step, a song in your heart, and a smile on your face. Try it! As people of God travelled up to the temple the procession would grow along the route, all merging into one joyful, praising crowd, having a wonderful time, celebrating the joy of the Lord. As Jesus rode into Jerusalem that first Palm Sunday, the crowd sang for joy those same psalms, welcoming Jesus, as Saviour and King. 'The crowds that went ahead of him and that followed were shouting, "Hosanna to the Son of David! Blessed is the one who comes in the name of the Lord! Hosanna in the highest heaven!"' (Matthew 21:9). There was an air of joy and celebration, with laughter and singing, releasing the gloom and sadness, because the people had caught the vision of deliverance of victory through him.

Today a modern hymn has also captured that same sense of deliverance and victory, based on those same words. 'This is the day that the Lord has made, we will rejoice, we will rejoice and be glad in it.' It is one of the most popular of modern hymns with all ages, the words and music perfectly matched. Easy to remember, easy to sing, even for the least musically inclined, and if you really can't sing then you can clap your hands or stamp your feet along to the beat, and why not? Isn't God's love worth celebrating, his victory worth shouting about? It is the fulfilment of the promise given by God to his people in Jeremiah: 'There shall once more be heard the voice of mirth and the voice of gladness, the voice of the bridegroom and the voice of the bride, the voices of those who sing, as they bring thank offerings to the house of the Lord' (Jeremiah 33:10–11). Think of a wedding celebration, and you can see, hear and feel the meaning of this verse.

Celebration, gladness, mirth—but do we see it today? How do those of us who claim to be filled with the joy of the Lord express that joy? Patrick Forbes in his book *The Gospel of Folly* writes, 'The whole notion that the gospel is about joy and laughter hasn't really been taken aboard by a Church preoccupied with structures, working parties and advisory committees, in short with its own survival.'

I must admit that as I look around at services and meetings I do not always get the feeling of joy, laughter and celebration. Maybe it is to do with the British 'stiff upper lip', the attitude that frowns upon tears either of sadness or of laughter. Of course our faith is a serious business, the most important part of life, but we can be serious without being gloomy, surely? In the church we are often our own worst enemies. What do people see as they watch us going into or coming out of church? Do they get a feeling of celebration, fun, joy that makes an outsider want to come inside and join in? Look around next Sunday!

Recently I experienced an evening of fun and laughter, the like of which I have hardly ever experienced in my life—and I have had plenty of fun and laughter in my time! My husband Peter, our daughter Alison and myself were part of a vast crowd of people who had come together to have fun. For almost five hours we laughed, and were still laughing as we came home, and have continued to laugh as we remember that night. I would like to have told you it was at a great Christian gathering, but no it wasn't. It was 'An evening of happiness with Ken Dodd and friends'. We sang, we waved, we laughed, led of course by the comedy genius, called Britain's King of Comedy, and some of his quotes are very scriptural, his stories pure parables. He says, 'I see every day as a new experience. Every day is a good day, but if you can't have a happy day yourself, then make someone else happy.' I think Jesus would have approved of that! Speaking about the value of live shows, Ken Dodd says, 'The live show is the best show there is, because everybody is part of it. There's nothing quite like laughter—it's a tonic, the universal language that everyone understands.' Surely every church service is 'a live show'—it is all about being truly alive in God's presence.

In June 1997 I was invited to become diocesan chaplain to the Mothers' Union in the York Diocese. The letter of invitation arrived while I was stuck in a hospital bed following an accident in Italy— not really a laughing matter. Yet as soon as I read the letter of invitation I knew it was right to accept, and I knew what I intended to do: make the Mothers' Union fun! Here was my challenge, and I was ready for it. In the November of that year I was commissioned as chaplain in York Minster, and preached at that service. I began by telling them about being interviewed on radio that week about my new appointment, and why I had taken it, and what I hoped to do. I had told the interviewer that being a member of the Mothers' Union was fun, and I intended to continue that fun element. Afterwards as we had a cup of coffee together he had said to me, 'Do you really think the Mothers' Union is fun? It's surely not the word that comes immediately to mind?' So I gave him some instances of the fun I had enjoyed with the Mothers' Union, and of the need I always felt to have that sense of fun.

As I recounted this in the Minster I saw some eyebrows raised, and then I saw the smiles and I knew we were going to be all right! I did go on to unpack the word 'fun', and talked about it being made up of faith, unity and nourishment: the essential ingredients for a life that knows real joy and shares it with others, which to me is what the Mothers' Union is all about. One of the sights that delights my heart is a procession of Mothers' Union banners, and as I look at the banners and read the inscriptions, I also look at those who are carrying them. I see faces that show faith and experience, service, loyalty, concern for others, and I also notice the laughter lines, the smiles, and the twinkle in the eyes, and I want to say to them 'I can see the real you, so be yourself, go on!' If only we would allow ourselves the release of fun and laughter we would do ourselves, and others, more good than we could imagine. As it says in the book of Proverbs, 'A cheerful heart is a good medicine' (Proverbs 17:22). Perhaps the author Henry Ward Beecher was remembering that verse when he said, 'Mirth is God's medicine.' So with God and some cheerful friends, life could be and should be a great deal better than we think is possible, and far more healthy!

I always enjoy reading the book of Ecclesiastes—'the preacher' with all his wonderful illustrations of life. Thousands of years divide his time and ours, and yet human nature does not change. We are basically the same, and can benefit from the wisdom of the years. Can you imagine a preacher today getting up in the pulpit and saying these words? 'So I commend enjoyment, for there is nothing better for people under the sun to eat, and drink, and enjoy themselves, for this will go with them in their toil through the days of life that God gives them under the sun' (Ecclesiastes 8:15). There is something for the journey there! We all have to go through sadness and sorrow, hard work, hard slog, times of difficulty—this is all part of life. We all know that, we all see it, but there is also given to us something to lighten the journey, put a spring in our steps, laughter in our mouths. It is the assurance that God is there with us and for us.

The people of Israel knew that, and hung on to that, even in the most dreadful times, not least during the terrible events of the Second World War and all that happened to the Jewish people. Christians have known this through two thousand years, through persecution and rejection, through suffering so awful that we can hardly bear to think about it. Such suffering still happens, even today, in some parts of the world. Christians are put to death because they are not ashamed to proclaim that they belong to Jesus Christ, and are proud to share his good news, whatever it costs them. Perhaps our problem is that we are afraid to laugh in case we are thought of as flippant. Maybe we are afraid to sing the Lord's praises in case we make a fool of ourselves.

When Jesus hung on the cross, dying, the leaders laughed at him with a different kind of laughter, as did the soldiers and even one of the criminals beside him. All with the same taunt: 'Are you not the Messiah? Save yourself and us!' That was cruel laughter, vicious taunting of a dying man, and yet Jesus took it and transformed it into victory, new life for all. He gave himself to save us, so we might know the joy of deliverance and victory, and be able to sing and laugh for joy. In heaven there will be plenty of laughter, singing, celebration and yes, sheer fun. I am sure of that, so why don't we start practising now?

Lord, Today is the day you have given us to rejoice and be glad
in, today we celebrate the joy of life, of love, of victory,
today we join in songs of praise,
today we can laugh in spite of all the world throws at us,
today we can have fun and repel the gloom of sin and death,
today we can step out happily towards our heavenly home, with
eagerness and confidence,
today we rejoice in the power of the Holy Spirit,
today, this very day is the day you have made,
we will rejoice and be glad in it!

CHAPTER 22

Give us this day our daily bread

JOHN 6:35

Jesus said to them, 'I am the bread of life.
Whoever comes to me will never be hungry, and whoever believes
in me will never be thirsty.'

The two-page colour spread showed some of the rich, famous and beautiful people, the 'household names', and told of their search for fulfilment. Some had found what they were looking for through reading the Bible, joining a church, becoming committed Christians, but most of those featured had gone into other religions, cults, mystical teachings, and to following gurus who promised transcendental enlightenment. Why this interest in something or someone beyond themselves and their success? 'So what do you do if you have it all? Fame, looks and a blue-chip portfolio? What do you do if you have millions of followers gagging for your every photo opportunity?' was the question posed by the magazine, going on to add that even these people have their worries: 'lives constantly overshadowed by the threat of earthquakes, fire, staff shortages and wrinkles'. They recognize that their grasp on life is very precarious, and very dependent on influences beyond their control. We do not have to be rich, famous or beautiful to have come to that conclusion, do we?

We all have our goals in life, the things about which we feel that if we obtain them, then life will be perfect, our worries will be over. There is a glow and a satisfaction to be had in striving for and obtaining success in life, a pride in a job well done. Winning the 'cap and gown' of the college graduate, raising a family, gaining a seat on the local council, athletic prowess, growing the biggest marrow or the most beautiful rose, or becoming 'slimmer of the year'. If we did not have our goals, our aims in life, it would be a dull and rather pointless existence. It is when these become the 'be all and end all' that we come unstuck, for we know, even if we do not admit it, that after the initial high, we feel there must be something more than this. The danger is that we can end up going after more of the same, and become taken over by the trinkets of life, the glittering prizes of human achievement. Those who make the colour supplements, along with us more ordinary mortals with our smaller ambitions, are mirrored in the pages of history by those who have asked the same questions, who longed for a peace and satisfaction beyond their grasp, beyond their human understanding or experience.

As we read the Bible, learn from the history of God's people, listen to the words of Jesus, then we will begin to discover clues. Pieces of the picture of life start to come together, make sense, and give us pointers to both the source and completion of our quest.

When Jesus was tempted in the wilderness to turn stones into bread, to use his power to satisfy his physical need, he answered, 'It is written, "One does not live by bread alone, but by every word that comes from the mouth of God"' (Matthew 4:4), quoting from Deuteronomy 8:3. When God commanded his people not to forget him as they became prosperous and entered into the good life he had promised them, he reminded them of the times when they were hungry and needy, and he had fed them with manna from heaven. They needed food to sustain them on their journey and he gave it to them, but they also needed God's guidance and strength to be the people he had created them to be. Divine nourishment enabled them to understand their purpose as well as their place in God's plan.

For all of us, the word 'bread' conjures up so many different pictures and experiences, far beyond the crusty white from the family baker or the economy white sliced from the supermarket. While it is a few years now since the long-running popular television series *Bread*, many of us will recall that family sitting round the table sorting out their day-to-day lives, and entering into deep theological and political arguments, all laced with that wonderful humour which is so much part of Liverpool's culture. *Bread* was all about life—and the word is used to mean all that makes living possible: our strength to 'earn a crust', the cash to buy the things we need to survive, the basics of life.

Jesus knew what it was like to be hungry, desperate for bread. He saw the needy all around him too, and he felt an empathy with them. When he was confronted with a huge hungry crowd, the question he asked was, 'Where are we going to buy bread for these people to eat?' He asked the question of his disciples to draw out from them their concern for their fellow men and women. You could call it their heartfelt response to human need, to the situation there before them. It is the same question, I would suggest, that he puts to us as we look out at our hungry world today. What is our answer? Is it to hold up our hands in horror at the prospect of doing anything, feeling it is all quite beyond us? Or is it to say, 'This is what we have got; it's not much, but…' In the account of the feeding of the five thousand it was the latter response that produced the miracle, something we do well to bear in mind when faced with seemingly impossible situations. Jesus took the gift of a boy's lunch, offered it up in thanksgiving to God, and all the hungry were fed with plenty to spare.

As I walked up and down garden paths during Christian Aid week, collecting in those envelopes, I said 'thank you' to God for each and every person who gave me their offering, and for the miracles that would be performed through those coins and notes. What I have found in collecting for Christian Aid and for other agencies is that often it is those who have least who give most. There are many modern-day instances of the boy who gave his dinner—and all of it at that! And while there are hungry people in the world we need to go on giving generously to ensure that the work of the aid agencies can continue—and that means for always.

Of course, human nature being what it is, the people fed miraculously by Jesus thought they had discovered the easy answer to all their problems: a free bread ticket for life—no wonder they wanted to make him king. But Jesus recognized their motives, knowing they wanted him because their stomachs were filled, not because he offered the bread of heaven, food for their souls too. As Jesus explained to them that he was indeed 'the bread of life', offering them his very life so they might live eternally, most drifted away; the Jews complained about him, and many of his followers turned away from him saying, 'This teaching is difficult. Who can accept it?' Bread here on earth: 'Yes please!'; the bread of life: 'No thank you'. Yet the two go together, and as those who follow the way of Jesus we need to see the social and the spiritual as being part and parcel of each other. To feed the hungry and to proclaim the bread of life is one and the same gospel.

Bread was to take on a very special significance as Jesus shared a loaf of bread, along with wine, in that last supper with his friends before he died. As he broke the bread and shared it with them he told them, 'Take, eat, this is my body', and as he poured the wine, 'This is my blood of the covenant which is poured out for many for the forgiveness of sins' (Matthew 26:26–27). Broken, poured out, to be shared and lived out.

We 'break bread together' as we share with one another in the ordinary everyday events of life, in our homes, with friends, in the community. We recognize each other's needs and each other's gifts, we give and we receive, with thankfulness for each other. We break bread together as we obey our Lord's command, 'Do this, in remembrance of me.' We come gladly in response to his invitation to feed on him in our hearts with thanksgiving. As the bread is broken with the words, 'We break this bread to share in the body of Christ,' we respond, 'Though we are many, we are one body, because we all share in one bread.' I always find those words so awe-inspiring as I glimpse yet again that miracle of the bread of life being offered, that personal invitation being extended to me and to all those who will accept that invitation. When I preside at the holy communion service I always hold up the cup and the bread and say, 'The Lord says "Come!"' for it is not my invitation, or the church's, but the Lord himself who says to all who will, "Come"!'

When the two weary and sad friends of Jesus trudged back home on the road to Emmaus, they had heard he had risen from the dead, but could not take it in. A stranger walked along beside them, and listened to them, explained the scriptures, helped them to understand that this was all part of God's plan, enabled them to see beyond their own grief and confusion—but the friends still did not recognize him. It was not until that stranger came in as their invited guest, took bread, and blessed and broke it before them, that they recognized him. Jesus had walked with them. He had given them what they needed: space, time, explanation, guidance, his company on the road. But then as they put out their hands to receive the bread, they knew he was no stranger but their friend, their Master, their Risen Lord. He had risen, he was with them, they knew that now for sure.

There are many times in my own life when all goes well, I am busy and happy, feeling on top of the world, quite confident that I can cope with anything or anybody. At other times I am, as it is said, 'my own worst enemy'. I just don't want to know, won't accept help or advice, plod along feeling lost, confused and alone. Yet in good times and in bad, success and abject failure, as I take bread from the shelf, or put it ready for a meal, I have this sense of a warmth, a presence, maybe the sort of feeling the friends described as 'Were not our hearts burning within us...' For bread has been touched for all time by the hands of God. His imprint is always there, whether we recognize it or not. But when I come, whether bouncily or wearily, to share in holy communion, I recognize the one who invites me, calls me, offering his life to me, and I can know and do know his presence. I receive the bread of life, and with great thankfulness.

I wish I could maintain that spiritual 'high', that life could always be like that moment, but it is not a permanent banquet— it would do us no good, would it? Bread for the journey, the bread of life, is given so we might travel each day with Jesus. The manna in the wilderness was given fresh each morning, not to be hoarded or stored, but used that day. Jesus taught us to pray, 'Give us this day our daily bread'—to learn to trust God for each day as it comes, not building up bread mountains or a supply of ready-wrapped spiritual boosters. Fresh each day, used and shared each day, sufficient for each day too. Yes, 'something for the journey'. What is more, someone to share the journey with us—that is, of course, if we will let him!

> *Jesus, bread of life, bread of heaven,*
> *feed me now, today, sustain me on my journey,*
> *and help me to trust you for tomorrow,*
> *and for all the tomorrows.*
> *Jesus, bread of life, bread of heaven,*
> *feed me now, and evermore.*

CHAPTER 23

Love is the key

I CORINTHIANS 13:4–8a

Love is patient; love is kind; love is not envious or boastful
or arrogant or rude. It does not insist on its own way; it is not
irritable or resentful; it does not rejoice in wrongdoing, but
rejoices in the truth. It bears all things, believes all things, hopes
all things, endures all things. Love never ends.

Whenever I hear this 'treatise on love' read or quoted, part of me wants to run away and hide, because I know that when it comes to measuring up to this standard I am an abject failure. It strikes through my defences and excuses, right to my heart, and what I would like to think of as my bright and shiny heart just crumbles away like an autumn leaf touched by frost. The words come to cut me down to size and make me realize that I just haven't got what it takes to measure up to this standard. There is something that holds me down, in spite of wanting to rise above my failings and inadequacies. I feel rather as I did when one day at a fair I had a go at a game of strength, ringing a bell with a hammer. You probably have seen these games—a giant thermometer with a light at the top which flashes if you hit hard enough. A bell rings as well, announcing to all that you are a success, but there is also a scale on that meter which shows whether you were a total failure, weak, medium, or good. When I did it, it just hovered around 'total failure' and I wished I had never tried!

I don't know whether they had games with hammers and bells in Corinth, but they certainly had a league table of gifts and abilities, of their own making, and there was a constant argument going on as to what exactly these gifts and abilities were, and who possessed them. Corinth was a vibrant, sophisticated, permissive city sea-port, and was like any such centre populated by a rich variety of people, together with those passing through as travellers, merchants, adventurers. It had the reputation as one of the wildest, wickedest places of its time. Yet Paul established a church there, for out of this amazing mix of people were those who responded to the good news of Jesus and began the new life together, drawing in others through the grace and power of the Holy Spirit. Although they had nothing in common naturally, as Christians they were drawn together, and given an identity, a vision, a hope for the future. But they were still young in faith and experience, and so found it hard working out their faith in that place, having to contend with all that was going on—the temptations, the diversions, the old life pulling them back. They wanted the best for themselves, wanted to be seen as superior Christians, 'know it all, have it alls'. So what *was* the best gift of all? That is what they wanted to know, and so Paul writes to them, describing the variety of gifts the Holy Spirit bestows on the church, and explaining that all the gifts, even those they thought very mundane and ordinary, were equally useful for building up the church, and for reaching out to others. Then he points them to *the* gift, the one they should all aim for, the gift that will never go out of date, fade or become obsolete—the gift of love. So to them, and to us, is given this great section on what love is all about. Love is defined, set out in everyday terms, and not only what it is, but also what it is not.

Did they get the message? Do any of us get the message? We see it as a wonderful ideal, but how can we attain it? Corinth may be far removed in time and distance from us, but some things never change! So is there anything that can change us? In Andrew Lloyd Webber's musical *Aspects of Love* there is a beautiful song called 'Love changes everything'. It speaks of love changing every aspect of our lives, bringing to them something glorious, lasting, beautiful, and after love nothing is ever the same. A picture of the power of love: but is it just a romantic notion or a real possibility?

Before we can give love, we need to know what it is all about, to have experienced it. One of the great tragedies of our time is that so many have no experience of what love is. They have not had the advantage of being brought up in a loving, stable home environment, have not had the loving support of friends, have not felt appreciated or wanted in a society which grows ever more selfish and grasping. What passes for love is often ill-disguised lust, seeing people only as consumer units, to be discarded when they can no longer add to the profits. So where is the love that changes everything, including basic human nature?

It was Oscar Wilde who wrote, 'Keep love in your heart. A life without it is like a sunless garden when the flowers are dead. The consciousness of loving and being loved brings a warmth and richness to life that nothing else can bring.' This reminds us that love is at the heart of living, of creation itself, of being alive. Love is— Jesus. He is love personified. 'God so loved the world that he gave his only Son, so that everyone who believes in him may not perish but have eternal life' (John 3:16). One of the best-known verses of scripture sets love in its true context: it comes from God, it is for anyone, and it is for all time. Love brought Jesus to our earth; love sustained him here, even on the cross; love overcame every obstacle, even sin, suffering and death; love is risen; love never ends.

The picture Paul gives us of love is a picture of Jesus, his life, his way, his gifting. If only it could be on prescription, put in capsule or liquid form to be taken three times a day after food! If only it could be boxed and labelled and made available at our local supermarket or store so we could purchase it when we needed it, keep a stock of it in the cupboard or freezer. If only we could grow it in our garden, or get the kit from the 'do it yourself' shop, if only... Then we could share it with others, then we could use it, then everything would be whole, healed, beautiful, new. We could capture it, never to let it go.

John, writing to some of the first Christians, said this: 'Beloved, let us love one another, because love is from God' (1 John 4:7). He then goes on to tell them, 'God's love was revealed among us in this way: God sent his only Son into the world so that we might live through him. In this is love, not that we loved God, but that he loved us and sent his Son to be the atoning sacrifice for our sins. Beloved, since God loved us so much, we also ought to love one another' (1 John 4:9–11). So there's the secret explained, the secret of love made plain. It is not that we try to reach up and make ourselves loving, but that God has already reached down to us, and given us all we need. No need for pills, packages or pounds. We don't need a penny, only an open heart and open hands to receive God's gift of love and to let him grow in our lives, to fill us with his love and overflow into those around us, into our world, wherever it is needed.

Does it work? Indeed it does! It changes people, it changes situations; it never ends, for it is constantly being replenished. Like the ginger beer plant that was so popular a few years ago, you find the more you give away the more you have. Love is experienced in the splendour of life, in fact it has been described as 'a many splendoured thing'. We find it in the joys and celebrations of life, a wedding, a new baby, in building a home, a family, a firm. In the splendour of achievement, success, star-studded evenings, displays of brilliance, when the applause rings out. It is equally, and maybe even more so, discovered in the darkness, in distress, when the tears flow, when all seems lost, and life is emptied of everything you hold dear. When there seems nothing and nobody to hold on to, there is still love, Calvary love, love poured out, love in the touch of an arm around your shoulder, the shared tears, the hand holding yours, the love that 'bears all things, believes all things, hopes all things, endures all things' (1 Corinthians 13:7).

Does love last? I have lost count of how many times I have preached on that passage from 1 Corinthians 13 at weddings, looking at the young—or not always so young—couple in front of me, who are so full of love for each other that they are almost bursting, and I have tried to explain that love is not just for today with all the excitement, the celebration and the finery, but for every day. And I have prayed that they might remain in God's love, and in love with each other, but sadly some of those marriages are already shattered. Love did not last, it was not sufficient, not strong enough to withstand the demands upon it. Yet I know of so many who have weathered the most awful storms, had to go through suffering, loss, trouble, and yet their love has grown and been strengthened as together they have lived out that treatise of love, the power of God's love in their hearts and lives, in their situation.

I see that love lived out in the lives of those who are afflicted by illness, handicaps, their own or their partner's or family member's. The love they have for one another enables them to cope with whatever life flings at them. I see that love in the lives of those who care for others, often sacrificially, without any thought for themselves, only the well-being of those they care for, even when they get little or no thanks or response. Love that fails, love that lasts— what makes the difference? Perhaps it is that for some love is conditional. There are limits set, either consciously or unconsciously. When love is unconditional, there are no limits set, and then it lasts, it strengthens, it grows, it bears fruit, as God's love has borne fruit through what happened on the cross, through that unlimited, unconditional love that was poured out for us. As we look at and receive that love, can we ever put a limit on our loving? Jesus said, 'This is my commandment, that you love one another as I have loved you' (John 15:12). His love changes everything, has changed everything, and will go on changing everything too. His love changes us—if we will let him. Our weak attempts at loving God, our neighbours and ourselves can by God's grace be transformed into something so beautiful, powerful and active that nothing can withstand it, for it will reflect his love wherever it touches, whomever it lights upon. As I think about God's great love for me, I echo William Cowper's words:

> *Lord, it is my chief complaint,*
> *that my love is weak and faint.*
> *Yet I love thee, and adore,*
> *O for grace to love thee more!*

William Cowper, 1931–1800

CHAPTER 24

Wait for it

HABAKKUK 2:3

For there is still a vision for the appointed time;
it speaks of the end, and does not lie.
If it seems to tarry, wait for it;
it will surely come, it will not delay.

I am not good at waiting. I have a low patience threshold—which, put bluntly, means I am very impatient. I equate waiting time as wasted time; I like to be getting on with life, rushing headlong into the next item on my agenda, pushing on regardless, so waiting around makes me feel frustrated. Like it or not, I spend a lot of time waiting. For trains, which seem to have a perverse delight in running late. In traffic queues, while the opposite lane seems to be running freely. At the checkout in the supermarket, asking myself why I always seem to get behind someone with a mountain of goods and a dodgy cheque card; or waiting for the call or delivery that has been overlooked. Yet I know from experience that soon the train will arrive, the road will clear, the customer in front will get sorted out, and the call or delivery will arrive. This is all part of the ebb and flow of life. The waiting I dread is when I do not know what the end will be. Sitting in the dentist's or doctor's waiting room, imagination running riot, wondering what I will be told, what is going to happen. I am not very brave in such places! Waiting for news of a loved one who is undergoing surgery, sitting beside the bedside of a friend who is dying: this is the kind of waiting that I sometimes find almost unbearable.

At other times, waiting is both exciting and pleasurable. Waiting for a friend at the station, waiting for 'curtain up' at the theatre, waiting for the bride to arrive at the church door, waiting for the family to come home, waiting to spring a surprise at a birthday party. Waiting then is eager anticipation, a foretaste of the joy to come. As I have got older, and maybe a little mellower, I have discovered that there is virtue in waiting, and have come to accept it as both necessary and valuable. I realize that my problem is not in waiting but in not knowing the outcome—that is what makes me ill at ease. If I am sure of what is going to happen, then even if I have to wait, I am content. Slowly I am learning how to use waiting time positively, and by that I do not mean filling it up, but going into it, rather like relaxing into a warm bath at the end of the day, relaxing into the assurance of God's love and purpose, letting go and letting be.

When I was at college, many years ago now, I was fascinated by a lecturer's frequent references to 'the little read prophets'. My imagination worked overtime, and I could see this jolly band of tiny red men chasing along, holding in their hands scrolls of prophecies, which they were intent on delivering. It was a while before I realized that he meant they were not often read, rather than that they were small red men. What I did discover was a wealth of wisdom contained in their messages, as relevant for today as for the people and situations of their own era. They were men who would speak out the word that had been given them from God, often to people who did not want to hear or understand. Yet they would without fear or favour hold to the given word, hold to God, all their days.

One of those prophets was Habakkuk. He gave his prophecies at a time when Babylon was so dominant that no one dared resist. In Judah, society was at an all-time low, morally and politically. There was no sign of hope for anything better, and yet Habakkuk knew that God was in charge. The sins of the people—be they the people of God or the oppressors—would not go unpunished, but even though dark days lay ahead, God could still be found and known. There was still a future for his people, even though they would have to wait a long time to realize it. Habakkuk waited in hope and with joy, saying, 'Yet I will rejoice in the Lord; I will exult in the God of my salvation' (Habukkuk 3:18). He had a vision for the end of waiting, knowing that 'it will surely come'. We have the picture of the watchman on the tower looking, watching, waiting, ready, looking for the sign of hope which would surely come, the good news of release and victory.

In the book of Lamentations we find the promise, 'The Lord is good to those who wait for him, to the soul that seeks him. It is good that one should wait quietly for the salvation of the Lord' (Lamentations 3:25–26). In our world today, a world as desperate as the world of Habakkuk with all its sin and discord, oppression and misery, we can hold to that for ourselves. We can wait with confidence for we know that the Lord's salvation has come. Jesus is Lord! Lord over fear, Lord over death itself, Lord of all time and eternity.

We can use our waiting time—even in the supermarket, on the station platform, stuck in a queue or by the telephone or bedside, anywhere— to reflect on and rejoice in our salvation, and in our 'sure and certain hope'. I find that the more I do this, the more I discover of God and his purposes, the more I am renewed and refreshed for whatever might lie ahead. It is not easy; it needs practice and discipline too.

One of the most memorable sermons I have ever heard was some years ago during a conference for people who, like myself, were involved in the business of communications. It was during an early morning communion service, and I looked forward to hearing the preacher, for he had a very fine reputation. When it came to the sermon, he said, 'We have come to this service to feed upon our Lord in word and sacrament. We have heard the word in the Gospel reading this morning, we will now feed upon it in silence.' I felt slightly annoyed. After all, I wanted to hear what the preacher had to say, and I could be quiet any time (or thought I could!). There was a distinct sound of shuffling in the congregation—obviously some were thinking like me, but in a moment or two silence came, a lovely, holy silence. Gradually there came a calm and a peace, a quiet, and into that the Lord spoke to me, and I am sure to everyone in that place. We were indeed fed, and as later we received the bread and wine, fed by the sacrament of holy communion, it was a celebration of knowing that 'the Lord is here, his spirit is with us'—and in us. A wise preacher, a memorable sermon, a time of waiting to be fed, and a banquet enjoyed.

In William Clemmon's book *Discovering the Depths* he writes of 'wasting time for God' and says:

> *Wasting time for God simply means learning to love slowing down, silence and solitude. It means living life out of a deep transcendent integration, and 'quiet centre' from which words are spoken and life is lived at a deep enough level so that actions are made, not as reactions to another's action, but as responses to the inner promptings of our interior dialogue with self and God.*

We are afraid of wasting time, aren't we? I know I am. It is as though we have to earn our keep in this world by keeping going. Yet this is not God's intention, not his measurement or value of the thing we call 'time'. We speak of giving 'quality time' to our loved ones, our special interests, our work, as though there was first or second class time. Surely God's time is always quality time, and whatever is happening in time, he gives it quality, for it is part of eternity—and when we realize that, life takes on a new dimension, whether waiting, working or wasting it!

> *Lord, You know how difficult I find waiting.*
> *I want to know it all now.*
> *Remind me that waiting is never wasted,*
> *for every moment is a gift,*
> *and time but a fragment of eternity on my way home to you.*

CHAPTER 25

Glory, glory, hallelujah!

JOHN 1:14

And the Word became flesh and lived among us,
and we have seen his glory, the glory as of a father's only son,
full of grace and truth.

The moment I hear or read the first verse of John's Gospel, 'In the beginning was the Word, and the Word was with God, and the Word was God...' I can feel a tingle at the back of my neck which spreads almost instantly through my body. Those words shake me to the core with pentecostal power, demanding that I listen, I hear, I receive the message afresh. Pictures, sounds and memories fill my mind, and at the centre of it all is God, the living Word, challenging, drawing, holding me in his hand. Inviting me to discover something new from this statement of eternal truth. It is the feeling of coming in from the cold and dark to warmth and light; from standing on the doorstep to being enveloped into a loving embrace of welcome, drawn into the celebration, and having a contribution to make to it. If I had to put a time and place to it then it would be Christmas Eve, the midnight celebration of holy communion, and 'the Christmas Gospel': the celebration of the Word, looking forward to the receiving of the sacrament, which is a unity, a oneness, a eucharist—a thanksgiving for 'the Word made flesh' given and received.

Those first few verses of the gospel describe the coming of God's Son into our world, so that we might see God's glory for ourselves. The *Logos*, the Word, the mind and expression of God in human form, the glory of God here, now.

In the Old Testament we have the picture of the *shekinah* glory of God, being seen in the cloud as God spoke to Moses. It was the glory settling on Mount Sinai described in Exodus 24:17—'Now the appearance of the glory of the Lord was like a devouring fire on the top of the mountain in the sight of the people of Israel.' When the tabernacle had been erected and equipped according to God's instructions then God's glory filled it, a sign that God would be with them, his glory be wherever they were, a visible presence and assurance of his continuing protection and guidance, the glory of his love for them. It was the glory of the Lord dwelling with them, the word *shekinah* conveying the picture of that dwelling presence of God.

So John's words '…and we have seen his glory…' would speak powerfully, for everyone knew what God's glory meant, and yet here was someone saying that we have seen it, in a person. Not just a presence, a power, but in human form. The same glory as displayed on Mount Sinai but now also here and for everyone. Then John goes on to give his account of the gospel—the good news of Jesus Christ, the glorious good news of God's grace and truth. Later on, Paul writing to the Corinthians puts it like this: 'For it is the God who said, "Let light shine out of the darkness" who has shone in our hearts to give the light of the knowledge of the glory of God in the face of Jesus Christ' (2 Corinthians 4:6). God's glory came to us in the person of Jesus Christ, his son.

Emil Jellinek commissioned the design of the Daimler Simplex car. He was on the board of directors of Daimler, amongst other interests. He went from strength to strength in the industry and built up a motoring empire. He had a daughter called Mercedes who was his greatest treasure, and he was so proud of her that he gained permission to name the Daimler Simplex after her. By 1902 the Mercedes trade name had acquired full legal protection, to be used for ever. Every Mercedes is a tribute not just to a company or a designer but to love. The biggest motor retailer in Britain carries many famous and prestigious names, but there is a name displayed which is not of a vehicle but of the chairman's young daughter, Victoria. Her name graces showrooms as an expression of her father's love for her, and I know of hers for him too. Mercedes and Victoria, both more precious than empires, their names proudly proclaimed for all to see. Two human stories which reflect something of the love of God for his son, Jesus Christ, and of the son for his father. The glory of God would be seen in Jesus Christ, plain for all to see, all who wanted to see and open their eyes and their hearts to him.

Jesus was born here on earth, lived in humble surroundings, followed an ordinary trade, was subject to the difficulties and restrictions of the life of his time and yet as he went about he reflected God's glory in what he said, what he did and what he was. But he also reflected God's glory in special signs, the first of which was at a wedding in Cana. Jesus was there with his friends and his mother as guests, enjoying the celebration. Then something happened that would have spoilt the party, marred the celebrations, brought shame on the bridegroom: the wine ran out. And Jesus performed his first miracle, by turning ordinary water into wine of the very best quality. It says, 'Jesus did this, the first of his signs, in Cana of Galilee, and revealed his glory; and his disciples believed in him' (John 2:11).

Jesus performed many miracles during his ministry, saved many desperate situations, brought healing and help, physically, mentally and spiritually, but the very first miracle was to ensure a village wedding was a success, to be a giver of joy in an ordinary everyday occasion. We do not even know who the young couple were, or their relationship with Jesus and his family and friends. They may have been only acquaintances, for when there was a wedding in the East everybody was invited. Yet they were special to him, they mattered, he wanted them to enjoy themselves, especially as they began their new life together. Plain common water turned into the best wine to give them joy to share, to remember, to bind them together in a special relationship through what Jesus had done for them.

When Jesus touches our lives, when he reveals his glory to us, he turns the ordinary everyday things into sparkling new life. He steps in and rescues us, and provides us with more than we could ever have imagined. There is an old hymn which is still sometimes sung at weddings, and perhaps holds far more meaning than some more trendy offerings. It says:

> O Saviour, guest most bounteous of old in Galilee,
> Vouchsafe today thy presence with these who call on thee,
> Their store of earthly gladness transform to heavenly wine,
> And teach them in the tasting, to know the gift is thine.

> John Ellerton, 1826–1893

Thank God for the human touch that gives a taste of glory in our lives! The signs he shows in so many and varied situations point always to God's glory. They are but signs of something far beyond our human imagining, but which we can glimpse and understand through seeing Jesus, meeting with him, and putting his words into practice in our own lives.

When Jesus took his friends, Peter, James and John, up the mountain, they little thought they were about to see Jesus transfigured, in glory with Elijah and Moses, seeing the glory of God for themselves—but they did. It was so marvellous they would have liked to stay there for ever, away from the problems of life. No more worries, no more talk about suffering and death, no more fear, no more anxiety. On the top of a mountain amid the glory, it was perfect, but the glory was only for a moment. They had to return to cope with life and death in the light of that experience, not as a way of escape from the present but holding it as a vision of the victory to come. The voice of God came to them out of the cloud, with the affirmation and instruction, 'This is my Son, the Beloved; listen to him!' (Mark 9:7).

When Jesus received the news that his friend Lazarus was ill, he told his friends, 'This illness does not lead to death, rather it is for God's glory, so that the Son of God may be glorified through it' (John 11:4). But when they arrived at Bethany, Lazarus was dead, in fact had been dead four days, and his body lay decaying in the tomb. Where was the glory in that? Jesus was too late, death had won the race. Yet then the impossible happened: from death and decay Lazarus was brought back; God's glory was revealed through his Son. Only a short time afterwards Jesus would be arrested, beaten, humiliated, nailed to the cross, and his dead body placed in a tomb. Where was the glory in that? Surely it all could have been avoided? But through that, God's glory was revealed in the greatest miracle of all. Jesus was not brought back to life for a time, given an extension of this life like Lazarus, but raised to new life, eternal life. And through his rising came the gift of eternal life to everyone who believed in him.

God's glory is still experienced today, in all sorts of ways, in all sorts of people and situations, and the greatest miracle is seeing someone come to new life, the miracle of a new birth! I have had the privilege of seeing that happen over and over again, and I never cease to be amazed, overcome by the glory of God in Jesus Christ's saving work right here today. Seeing lives changed, seeing glorious things happen that I could never have dreamed of, getting glimpses of God's glory in faces and lives of people around me, situations transformed, hopelessness turned to celebration.

On a beautiful day in summer, looking out at a peaceful sunlit landscape, I find it easy to recognize the glory of God. It is there, spread out before me. But on a wet, cold winter's day, what is there to see? Only the clouds, and the murky, brief winter light. Time and time again as I ponder on this scene, and long for light, for a touch of glory, it comes. A sudden shaft of sun breaks through, lighting up just for a moment a patch of grass or a frosted bush, and I know it as a sign—a sign that God's glory is still there, even though I may not see it or feel it.

Through sunlight and winter's gloom, God's glory shines. At celebrations and in dire suffering and through death, God's glory shines, and as we look to Jesus we can see it and experience it for ourselves, and begin to discover something of what Paul meant when he spoke of 'Christ in you, the hope of glory' (Colossians 1:27). To pray in the words of Charles Wesley:

> *Finish then thy new creation,*
> *pure and spotless let us be,*
> *Let us see thy great salvation,*
> *perfectly restored in thee.*
> *Changed from glory into glory,*
> *till in heaven we take our place,*
> *Till we cast our crowns before thee,*
> *lost in wonder, love and praise.*

CHAPTER 26

You can't help worrying —or can you?

LUKE 12:22–23

'Therefore I tell you, do not worry about your life, what you will eat, or about your body, what you will wear. For life is more than food, and the body more than clothing.'

I picked up the book in one of those remainders and oddments bookshops, and I paid sixty pence for it! It was a book of some of the sketches and songs by the writer and actor Joyce Grenfell. Although it is some years now since she died, her material is as fresh, amusing and moving as if it had been written today. She had the gift of capturing human nature with deadly accuracy, but always in a kindly way, making those characters come alive with humour, pathos, and with the ability to take a dig at an unsuspecting audience. One that found its target in me, as I suspect with many other people too, was entitled 'A Terrible Worrier'. The problem with Mrs Moss—the terrible worrier—was all to do with a rabbit, a dead one, with fur on, which she had won in a raffle. The raffle had turned into a nightmare for our terrible worrier. First of all, in case she won the first prize of a cruise, in case she was made to go on it, and the ship sank, and the council heard she had gone on a cruise and put her rent up, and... In the end she wins a rabbit, but that to her is as much a problem as the cruise, which incidentally she didn't win! Trying to dispose of the rabbit caused her terrible worry, resulting in a sleepless night and needing the advice of her solicitor, or thinking she did. She had nothing to worry about at all, but being 'a terrible worrier' everything blew up out of all proportion. But then Mrs Moss didn't exist—she was merely a figment of Joyce Grenfell's imagination, or was she? I meet the like of Mrs Moss all the time, and there is quite a lot of Mrs Moss in me!

Jesus told a parable of a farmer who had such a great harvest, he worried what to do with it all. The story was in response to a request by a man so worried he wasn't going to get his fair share of the family inheritance that he wanted Jesus to tell his brother how to divide it. Jesus made it very clear that he was not in the business of sorting out those kinds of problems! The parable of the rich farmer who died before he could enjoy the profits of his harvest was a sharp reminder to the man worried about his inheritance and to us as well—a reminder that we need to get our priorities straight. It is often glibly said, 'You can't take it with you'. True enough, but Jesus said we do take a record of our deeds, our attitude to and use of possessions, which we may think of as ours, but in fact are only tools of our stewardship here on earth.

Today we seem to spend so much of our time and energy worrying about protecting our possessions, holding on to what we have got, making sure our investments are watertight, our pension rights tied up. Our natural predisposition to acquiring and holding on to what we call our assets is fuelled by relentless powerful advertising, offering us complete security in every aspect of our life at a price. Of course we need to be sensible, to be good stewards of what we have, and not to put temptation into the way of others, but the question we have to ask ourselves is, 'Do I possess things, or do things possess me?' Mrs Moss was possessed by a rabbit, the farmer by his crop yield, and all they gave in return was a load of worry!

One of the great problems of life today is that we expect, even demand, absolute security and safety. If we do not get it then someone is held to be responsible, and must be sued in court for failing to meet our expectations. We are very strong on our rights, but often so weak in understanding and sympathy. 'Making allowances' seems to have no place in our society, and what does this attitude to life result in? Sleepless nights, ulcers, stress, and a load of worry which saps our energy, destroys our peace of mind, and robs us of our enjoyment of life. The tragedy is that it is self-inflicted, for there is no need for us to suffer like this. We can be free of this killer disease, we can know real peace and security.

The bestselling writer Dale Carnegie once said in an interview, 'If only the people who worry about their liabilities would think about the riches they do possess, they would stop worrying. Would you sell both your eyes for a million dollars… or your two legs… or your hands… or your hearing? Add up what you do have and you'll find that you won't sell them for all the gold in the world. The best things in life are yours, if you can appreciate yourself. That's the way to stop worrying, and start living!'

Worrying about what we have got, or what we haven't got, does no good. As Jesus said, we need to realize that life itself is precious, the greatest gift of all. The rest are mere trappings, and very disposable and fragile trappings at that!

The other day I was sitting in the grounds of Chatsworth House in Derbyshire, enjoying a picnic in the sunshine, looking across at the imposing house, and the glorious parkland. Nearby a couple were having their picnic beside their car, and I got into conversation with them, commenting on what a beautiful day it was, and what a lovely spot Chatsworth was. The woman looked at me, and pointed across to the house, saying sharply, 'It's all right for some, isn't it? Having all this, born with a silver spoon in their mouths. We have had to work for every penny we've got. I'd like to be in their shoes, they have no worries like us ordinary folk.' My response to them, and I hope I managed to say it kindly, was, 'We are here enjoying the same fresh air, the same view, being able to appreciate the beauty of this place just as much as though we owned it. We have to be thankful that they have opened up their home to us, and I am sure it's not easy being responsible for the upkeep of it all. It must be hard work.'

The response was a reluctant sort of grunt, and shortly after they left without a word. I found it sad that they were able to look at such a lovely view on a beautiful day and, instead of being thankful, were envious and judgmental. I thought of some of the people I know who, through age or illness or because of their handicaps or difficulties, are unable to get outside to enjoy the view, smell the fresh air. Yet they are so grateful for simple little things, take such a delight in sharing what they have and rejoicing in the opportunities and achievements of others. They have learned to appreciate each moment, are able to sit light to the things so many of us try to protect and hang on to as the means of our existence. As one old lady said to me recently, 'I'm not frightened of tomorrow. God has got it all in hand, that's good enough for me, and anyway, no one can rob me of what I have got—my memories, my faith, and all the love and prayer that's around me. I've nothing to be worried about. God is good!' She has a wonderful treasury to dip into, and she delights in sharing it too! It is worth far more than cruises, barns, houses or investments. Because she has learned the true value of life, she is safe and secure and rejoices in it every day. It is a present reality, not just something for the future.

The reason we do worry about the future is perhaps that we feel we will not be able to cope with what might happen. It is to do with 'saving for a rainy day', being protected against adversity. So we worry about our health, our faculties, our job, our pension, our physical and financial strength. I can almost see Jesus smiling a wry smile, shaking his head at our lack of faith, while lovingly stretching out his hand to us as he says, 'Do not worry about tomorrow, for tomorrow will bring worries of its own. Today's trouble is enough for today' (Matthew 6:34). Life is set out in manageable chunks, a day at a time, and if we are sensible we will take it a day at a time too.

As I look at my diary, the commitments I have made, I worry whether I will be able to do it all, as though I was some sort of superstar, and everything depended on me! This is both arrogant and ridiculous, and maybe I deserve to lose sleep through worrying about it all. What I have found is that if I sit down and review what I need to do today, and get on with that, then it works out. Why take up the burdens of tomorrow? After all, everything could be changed by tomorrow, and so what is the use of worrying about it?

But it is more than this. It is not just about tomorrow, and however many tomorrows there might or might not be. It is about recognizing who is at the centre of life, who is in control, who holds the key to the future. The antidote to worry is trust. When I feel I am in danger of being overwhelmed by worry and anxiety, I hold on to this verse: 'Cast all your anxiety on him, because he cares for you' (1 Peter 5:7). In other words, 'Drop it—leave it— God knows, and cares, and it's all right!'

Another of the pieces in my 60p Joyce Grenfell book is entitled 'Time' and it finishes with the words, 'There is no such thing as time, only this very minute, and I'm in it, thank the Lord.'

Thank the Lord indeed! Today, tomorrow, time and eternity are all in his hands, and so am I, and so are you. Stop worrying, trust him, and thank him, and sleep well!

Lord, Forgive me for thinking life depends on me, and for trying to safeguard my future by accumulating, scheming, worrying, planning, and losing sleep over things that do not matter. Help me to recognize what is important, and what is not, to set my mind, heart and will on knowing and loving you, and so finding fulfilment in your service, enjoying the peace and freedom that are your gift to me for today and always.

CHAPTER 27

Capture the vision

REVELATION 4:1–2

After this I looked, and there in heaven a door stood open! And the first voice, which I had heard speaking to me like a trumpet, said, 'Come up here, and I will show you what must take place after this.' At once I was in the spirit, and there in heaven stood a throne, with one seated on the throne.

Late afternoon in January. The weak, watery sunlight that had been filtering through the stained-glass windows earlier in the day had now been replaced with a grey light. Now and again the fading sun tried to stab through, but with little success. Soon it would be dark, and I would be on my way home after a day spent as 'chaplain on duty' in York Minster.

I always enjoy being in the Minster, and see my day a month as one of the Honorary Chaplains as a privilege and pleasure. I have the opportunity to meet people from all over the world who come into the Minster. I can listen to them, often pray with and for them, giving them a chance to share with a stranger things that maybe they would find hard to share with someone close. Often it is just after I have taken the prayers on the hour, or following the mid-day holy communion service, that someone will come up and hesitantly say, 'Could I have a word with you, please?' and then share something on their hearts at that time. Again and again they will say that it was being in the Minster, feeling a sense of God's presence, that made them want to share with someone there and then how they felt.

On that particular January day there had been fewer visitors than usual. The rush begins with the coming of spring, through the summer months, and into the autumn, but the short dark days of winter are not so enticing. Yet the Minster looked very different, felt very different that day. It was not just that there were fewer people around, but the fact that the nave was completely cleared of all its furniture. No roped-off areas, no rows of seats, just clear space, giving a feel of how the Minster had been many years ago, a sense of powerful spaciousness, uncluttered and unhindered. I found myself noticing things of which I had never been conscious before, enjoying those hidden treasures and feeling very thankful that for the month of January the Minster would remain like this, giving people that experience, and the freedom and space to explore it.

Now, as my day was almost over, I was walking down the south aisle with John, one of the vergers, heading for a welcome cup of tea together. All of a sudden we saw a small girl, aged about five or six, walking on tiptoe down the centre of the nave. Her arms were outstretched, and she was gazing with a rapt expression towards the entrance to the choir, where a visiting group of singers were rehearsing for evensong. Her tiny figure was dwarfed by the vastness of space, and yet was so much the centre of it. She radiated wonder, joy, anticipation and discovery. We stood, almost holding our breath at the sight of her—caught up in the wonder of space and light, oblivious of anyone or anything else. Then John said to me very quietly, 'If only we could capture that!' We envied that child, for she had glimpsed something far greater, far more wonderful than we had ever done, although we thought we knew this building, knew what it was all about. Yet through her spontaneous response she shared her vision with us. We too were caught up into the presence of something even greater than the Minster itself, into the presence, beauty and power of God.

In the book of Revelation we are introduced to something beyond our experience and understanding. Awe-inspiring, frightening, confusing, too much to take in with our earthbound reasoning, and so often we ignore it, skip over it, even dismiss it, rather than open ourselves to it. John, exiled on the island of Patmos, was earthbound all right, stuck in that bleak, inhospitable place. He would have all the time in the world to look back on his life, remembering the years he had shared with Jesus, all the amazing happenings. Remembering what had happened after the death of Jesus, and after his resurrection and ascension too. The excitement, the hope, the joy, and the expectation that Jesus would soon return in glory and power, to take the believers to heaven—and it had just not happened.

The initial mushrooming of churches devoted to their Lord and Saviour, and responding to the teaching and practical application of the gospel, had been marred by disputes amongst Christians. Commitment wavered, and persecution had picked them off. John, in exile, would have had many questions as he remembered the promises of Jesus and his own experiences, when now it seemed to be all falling apart. But he was steadfast in faith, filled with the Holy Spirit, and was looking eagerly for a sign, for light, for a word—and it happened. The door was opened to give him a glimpse into heaven, into the future, and it was given not just for him to enjoy, but to record and pass on.

What a revelation! How could anyone record in words something beyond words? The translation of the vision, the revelation into human terms could not be adequate, but it could capture the spirit of it. In a small way our experience in York Minster that January afternoon was like that. Impossible to put into words just what that vision was, what that child who was the open door into heaven for us showed. I have to be content to say, 'It was like…' and as John the verger put it, 'If only we could capture that!' If only! We couldn't, but we could feel it, and for a brief moment be part of it, and remember it, and try to share it. Of course John on Patmos was not the only one to have a vision, an open door into heaven. Scripture is shot through with such experiences, and while they all are different, they have a unity. Many record a time and a place. For Isaiah it was: 'In the year that King Uzziah died, I saw the Lord sitting on a throne, high and lofty, and the hem of his robe filled the temple' (Isaiah 6:1). The immediate response of Isaiah was of total shock and blind terror. Faced with the absolute purity and holiness of God, he recognized his own sinful state, and that of the community of which he was part. Yet touched by the fire of God's forgiveness and enabling love, he could then respond to the call to be God's mouthpiece, and know the divine power to fulfil his calling.

Stephen, speaking before the council, witnessing to his Lord, was encouraged by a vision. 'Look,' he said, 'I see the heavens opened and the Son of Man standing at the right hand of God.' The response of those who heard him was to cover their ears. They didn't want to hear or see, and they destroyed, or thought they did, the one who had shared with them the vision. Yet the vision sustained Stephen in death, and in his final moments he could cry out, 'Lord Jesus, receive my spirit' and in a prayer for forgiveness for those who closed their ears and hearts, 'Lord, do not hold this sin against them' (Acts 7:56, 59–60). One man standing there witnessing all this could put a time and place to it: Saul, the one who approved of the killing not only of Stephen but of all Christians. He saw that as his purpose in life, yet later he would also see a vision, a life-changing, name-changing vision, after which Saul the persecutor became Paul the apostle, the visionary, missionary, teacher, disciple of Jesus Christ. The vision was to be the starting-block for the race of faith, and Paul would boldly witness, 'I was not disobedient to the heavenly vision' (Acts 26:19) as he, like Stephen and countless Christians after him, was brought to account for his faith.

It is easy to read and marvel at the visions given in scripture, to stand in awe of those who not only saw visions, but recorded them and lived them out in their lives. Standing on the edge of a new millennium, we have enough to do making sense of today, without being caught up in visions. Leave that to the leaders, 'the powers that be', those who know about such things. Yet ordinary people are getting a vision, are stepping out in faith, and working out that vision in practical everyday terms.

God opens doors so that saints and sinners, the great and the good, the very ordinary and the 'black sheep' too might see something beyond their wildest imagining, see beyond themselves, see not only possibilities, but the glorious reality that not only lies in the future, but is present right now.

As I look back on my life and all its amazing twists and turns, the doors that have opened, I can only thank God for every moment he has given me. It is often in the ordinary everyday things that God opens up a door of vision and opportunity, at a time when we least expect it. We cannot keep hold of it, but we can go through it and discover a whole new world, a foretaste of heaven that will resound beyond ourselves into eternity.

> *Awaken me to your presence,*
> *alert me to your love,*
> *affirm me in your peace.*
> *Open to me your way,*
> *reveal to me your joy,*
> *enfold me in your light.*
> *For my heart is ready,*
> *Lord, my heart is ready.*

David Adam, *The Open Gate*

CHAPTER 28

Nearer God's heart
in a garden

ISAIAH 58:11

*The Lord will guide you continually, and satisfy your needs
in parched places, and make your bones strong; and you shall be
like a watered garden, like a spring of water, whose
waters never fail.*

The picture of a watered garden is one that evokes deep feelings, not only in keen gardeners but in city-dwellers, wanderers, the dispossessed, and homeless. It is a picture of heaven, of stability, beauty, peace, safety, refreshment, of all that would satisfy human longings. To have a garden, enjoy it, tend it, is probably one of the deepest-seated desires in many of us, and even for those who profess to hate gardening, there is still the enjoyment of looking at gardens, enjoying the result of others' hard work!

The essayist Francis Bacon (1561–1626) wrote, 'God Almighty first planted a garden, and indeed it is the purest of human pleasures.' In the story of creation we see God with a magnificent sweep bringing into being the heavens and earth, day and night, the sea and the sky, sun and moon, through his power and might, filling the wide canvas with vibrant colours and textures and every form of life, including human beings. It is extravagant, dramatic, awe-inspiring, the work of God, the Almighty, everlasting God. Then we see the gentle human face of God: God the gardener, planting within this huge universe a plot—a garden, a place for him to enjoy the company of men and women, to be partners in the garden, share in it, enjoy it together. A place where God and his human creatures could be at home together, creator and created, as friends. 'The Lord God planted a garden in Eden, in the east, and there he put the man whom he had formed' (Genesis 2:8). The perfect garden scheme, ever-changing, watered, constantly renewed, providing everything needed to satisfy body, mind and spirit. Food, beauty, companionship—what more could anyone ask for? Perhaps it was this that inspired poet Dorothy Gurney

(1858–1932) to write those words, so beloved of gardeners and garden lovers:

The kiss of the sun for pardon,
the song of the birds for mirth.
One is nearer God's heart in a garden,
than anywhere else on earth.

For God's heart was in that garden, created by his power, sustained by his love, and given as a gift to the first man and the first woman, with one proviso: there was one fruit that must not be taken. All was there to be enjoyed, but for the fruit of this tree, the rule was 'look but do not take'. The story of Adam and Eve is well known— 'the fall' that affected all creation, all life. The beguiling voice of the serpent made it seem so very advantageous to disregard God's instruction. Surely there was everything to gain and nothing to lose? The woman needed little persuading, the man neither. How enjoyable it was—but what about the consequences? In vain the man blamed the woman and the woman the serpent, but each had disobeyed and must now suffer the consequences. They had broken the law of God, they had broken the relationship between them, and Eden could be no longer their home or their refuge. They were sent out into the world to fend for themselves, to wander, toil, suffer, die, to pass on to those who came after them the disease of sin. And yet God loved them, and was planning a rescue mission to bring back men and women into the relationship that had been marred by disobedience.

As they wandered through the years of history, through deserts, slavery, oppression, persecution, God never let them go. He provided for them as his people, giving them leaders, teachers, prophets. He sustained them, even though time and time again they disregarded his word, rejected his prophets, and ran after other gods of their own making. Yet always he rescued and renewed them, holding out before them the promise of a new life, a heavenly garden city, an inheritance, to be at home with him for ever. Then, when the time was right, he sent his son to complete the mission. As John Henry Newman's hymn puts it, 'O loving wisdom of our God, when all was sin and shame, a second Adam to the fight, and to the rescue came.' Jesus came to restore that relationship between God and his people, to bring us back from sin, disobedience and death. It was no easy option: Jesus was sub-ject to temptation, not least to avoid suffering, humiliation, death. It was in another garden, the garden of Gethsemane, that Jesus prayed, 'My Father, if it is possible, let this cup pass from me; yet not what I want but what you want' (Matthew 26:39). He asked his friends to support him through that ordeal, but they failed him, sleeping while he agonized, yet he did not fail them, or his Father.

When I was in the Holy Land I visited the reputed site of the garden of Gethsemane, with its ancient olive trees. It seemed so drab, so ordinary, with nothing particularly attractive about it. Yet as I thought there about what Jesus had endured in the garden of Gethsemane, it became for me beautiful, radiant, rich with mean-ing. As I stood there with other pilgrims from all over the world we were silenced by the overwhelming feeling of a presence and power. Unable to speak, we made our way quietly from that place.

Jesus was obedient. He did walk the way of the cross, did suffer and die—for us, for all people, past, present and future. As Newman's hymn continues, 'O wisest love, that flesh and blood, which did in Adam fail, should strive afresh against the foe, should strive and should prevail.'

It was in a garden that his body was laid by two secret disciples, Joseph of Arimathea and Nicodemus. They had come to know and accept Jesus, but had been afraid to commit themselves to him openly, frightened of the consequences. But after his death they found the courage and strength to ask for his body, and give it an honourable burial in the garden tomb. They acknowledged him in death, offering their services, just as the women did when they came to the tomb, and when Mary remained there, held by love and grief, mourning for him. It must have been a sombre place, a place of tears, regrets, desolation. Then all was changed. No longer a dead body enclosed, but an empty tomb, a risen Lord! When Jesus spoke to Mary she thought he was the gardener, someone there to look after the place, but when he spoke her name, she knew it was her Lord and Master, her friend, who had died but was now alive—and for ever. The garden of sadness, of death, became the place of new life, resurrection, of love and power. Not a place to stand and weep in, but to run from with joy, excitement, taking the good news to those who would hear. Many did find it very difficult to take in, to believe, but it was—and is—true. The Lord is risen—risen indeed!

When I was in the Holy Land, I visited the ancient Church of the Holy Sepulchre, revered as the place of the tomb, and also the Garden Tomb, set in a most beautiful garden just outside the Damascus Gate and kept so that people can come and be quiet, and share in worship amid trees, shrubs and flowers of the Bible. I have to admit, though, that I felt interest, but no real sense that either was the place. I did feel sad about that, as I saw around me so many people who were having deep spiritual experiences—I could see that by their faces, their posture, the sound of their prayers. I was left out—or so I thought. I wanted to be one of them, and yet it was not for me. But as I read again the account of the resurrection appearances, the message of the angels came to me as personally as though we were face to face. 'Why do you look for the living amongst the dead? He is not here, but has risen!' (Luke 24:5). The place of the tomb was secondary, wherever it might or might not be. What mattered was the realization, the joy, that the Lord had risen, and that I had received the message. I knew it was true, and I had also been entrusted with sharing the good news. I did not need to be in Jerusalem to know or do that, because it is for all time, and everywhere.

It was some time later, after I had returned from the Holy Land, that I was reading Isaiah 58. I read the promise of God to satisfy needs in parched places and I remembered my sadness in trying to find a Garden Tomb experience, while all the time the garden experience was there, within me. 'You shall be like a watered garden' (v. 11)—watered, brought to life through God's word, through the knowledge of the risen Lord, touched by angels—what more did I need?

In the last chapter of the last book of the Bible, Revelation 22, we have the picture of heaven, of Eden restored. A garden city, new Jerusalem, with God's promise fulfilled and the gates held wide open for all those who will enter. As a river flowed through Eden to water the garden, so the river of the water of life flows through the city, through every part, nourishing, providing everything needed to promote health and happiness. The tree of life is there, providing fruit, not forbidden but given, a wonderful variety changing each month, and 'the leaves of the tree are for the healing of the nations' (Revelation 22:2). Beauty, nourishment, healing, and the relationship restored between God and men and women. 'Nearer God's heart in a garden...' Surely we are *in* his heart in the garden. Eden, Gethsemane, the garden of the empty tomb, and finally new Jerusalem, with its gates flung wide, welcoming us home to God, to his heart, through his Son, 'who for the sake of the joy that was set before him endured the cross, disregarding its shame, and has taken his seat at the right hand of the throne of God' (Hebrews 12:2).

God was there at the beginning, there through the suffering, through death and resurrection. And he is with us now, planning to welcome us back home so that we can enjoy his company, in the presence of his son. We can live that life in the spirit together with all his people. Together in the garden city, renewing friendships, working and praising together, and discovering for ourselves the life that God always intended for us, which we glimpse here on earth, but will then enjoy forever.

> *O blessed is that land of God,*
> *where saints abide for ever,*
> *where golden fields spread far and broad,*
> *where flows the crystal river.*
> *The strains of all its holy throng,*
> *with ours today are blending,*
> *thrice blessed is that harvest song,*
> *which never hath an ending.*

William Chatterton Dix, 1837–1898

CHAPTER 29

Time—friend or enemy?

PSALM 71:17–18

O God from my youth you have taught me,
and I still proclaim your wondrous deeds.
So even to old age and grey hairs,
O God do not forsake me,
until I proclaim your might
to all the generations to come.

The young reporter had phoned me for some information about a church event in which I was involved. She apologized for having to ask how to spell my name: 'I'm new here, and I haven't got to know people yet.' I assured her that it was quite all right, I was used to seeing all sorts of spelling of my name, and she was much more sensible to ask than add to the list of variations. We chatted on and checked she had the information she required, then she said, 'Oh, one final question, Mrs Cundiff. How old are you?' I felt myself bristle, and then said, rather sharply, 'And what has that got to do with it? I don't think it's relevant.' She hastily agreed, but added, 'It is just one of the questions we always ask.'

As I replaced the phone and walked into the kitchen to make myself a cup of coffee, I realized it was the first time I had ever responded like that. Whenever I had been asked my age I cheerfully gave it, until today—so why the difference? Maybe it was because that morning I was feeling a bit under par, and as I had looked in the mirror and caught sight of the grey hairs, I had remembered some words of my mother, a few years before she died. She hated growing old—she had a young, active mind, and felt imprisoned in a body which was suddenly beginning to slow down. She said to me, 'I look in the mirror and I see an old woman, and I don't like it!' Now I knew what my mother had meant, and I had every sympathy with her feelings.

I decided to take my coffee outside, sit on the seat in the sunshine, look at the garden, remind myself how good life was, and how grateful I ought to be. Again I asked myself why the reporter's question had touched me on the raw. I thought back over the last few days. I had spent quite a lot of time with the elderly, some of them quite ill. I had visited people in two nursing homes and some in sheltered accommodation. I had witnessed some of the pain and discomfort age brings, the sadness of those who had to give up their own homes 'to be looked after', and saw the decline not only of bodily power but mental ability too—the slow responses, the forgetfulness, lack of concentration in those who I remembered as so lively and active only weeks, months, years ago. How long? Time passes so quickly. When was it...?

I remembered the fun of being sixty. The party, the jokes, the 'who would think you were sixty?' remarks, which I found flattering, even if I had the suspicion they might just be humouring me. I rejoiced in being able to get a Senior Citizen Railcard, avail myself of travel tokens, and enjoy concessions at the theatre or in visiting exhibitions, gardens, country houses. Only the week before, having a day out with my daughter, I had laughed with her at the bill which read, 'One haddock and chips and one "Golden Oldie"' and had tucked the bill into my purse to show others the benefits of being a 'golden oldie'. I picked up a book from my shelf in which I had contributed a piece on being sixty and thought, 'And that's six years ago now.' Perhaps I was beginning to feel my age, and on reflection realized that no one asked me if I was entitled to concessions these days. They just gave them to me, so it was obvious I looked over sixty, and lately a number of people had casually asked me if I was thinking of retiring yet. It was a raw spot, and that reporter had touched it and made me jump!

Did I fear old age? Perhaps becoming like some of those I visited, being restricted, hemmed in, when there was so much I still wanted to do, so many challenges yet to meet, places to go, things in the future I wanted to be part of and accomplish. Age had never seemed a problem until today.

Then some words of Psalm 71 came into my mind, and I thanked God I still had a good memory, for some things anyway! I went back into the house, got my Bible and then took it back out into the garden, sat down and found the psalm. It was headed 'Prayer for lifelong protection and help' and I began to pray it through slowly, taking each verse and meditating on it. We do not know the author of this psalm—whether it was David or not we are not told—but what comes through is that the author is feeling his age too. He expresses his concern about growing old, and concern for his future. He had known a lot of trouble in his life, it had been a battle, but he had come through. What now, when his strength was failing? What would happen?

He looks back over his life, recognizing that God had been there right from the beginning: '...it was you who took me from my mother's womb...' (v. 6). He had known God's presence and strength all his days. He had leaned on the Lord, found support and help, had known success, had been revived over and over again, enabled to proclaim the word of the Lord, sing his praises, rejoice in him. He had been able to share the good news of God's love and power with others, he had been honoured and comforted, been able to overcome problems, confound unbelievers, delight in giving his testimony of what God had done for him, and he could point others to that God who would care for them too. He could shout from the housetops that God is faithful, God is the God of power and righteousness, God reigns, God cares, God would never let him go. He asks God to help him, he affirms his faith in the God who rescued his soul. As I read and prayed that psalm I knew the same feelings, fears and emotions as the writer. I also knew the same hope and confidence in our God who from our mother's womb to old age is right there, and always will be.

As I closed my Bible and looked across the sunlit garden, I praised God for everything he had done in my life, everything he had enabled me to do, and everything he would continue to do, however many grey hairs appeared, or however quickly my faculties declined. I thought of those who were such a support to me in my life and ministry, people of all ages, but especially some of those 'elderly' folk who were a constant source of wisdom and encouragement, whose prayers upheld me, whose love was strong and firm. Many of them were confined to their home or even a room in a nursing home, but having as effective a ministry as that of any other person in the church.

I re-read the words I had written just after my sixtieth birthday:

> ... but there are advantages in growing older. The years have taught me lessons. I have kept old friends, and made new ones... what about God? What does he think of me at sixty? 'Do not be afraid. I will save you. I have called you by name. You are mine.'

His promise is as true today as it was yesterday, and will be for all my tomorrows. He is my Father, and I am his child forever… I have nothing to fear. For I am safe and secure, and always will be.

Six years on—how do I feel now? Well, I can still say that, know that and rejoice in it. I can identify with the psalmist too, can make his words my own, and I thank God for that elderly psalmist who, like me, found growing old a problem, until he looked away from himself to the God who knew and loved him always, at every stage of his life.

One of my favourite posters has a bright yellow sunflower on it, with the words, 'Blossom where you are planted'. I have always interpreted that as being content to be where you are, rather than looking longingly somewhere else. It could mean getting stuck in to the present opportunities and challenges rather than what might have been or might yet be. I still say 'Amen' to that, but maybe as I face up to the years' passing, to what might be seen as my 'sell by date', I realize that to blossom where you are planted not only means place but time. There are things I can do, experiences I can use, even advantages I have gained which are just right for today. I am the right person at the right time—and who knows what that could result in? My job is not to probe, reason, or even complain, but to enjoy and accept it.

I think of a couple who came to our church just two or three years ago, following their retirement to the area. They have made such a difference to our life as a church, as a fellowship. They are two of the greatest gifts God has given to us, and they came at just the right time. We needed them, and God sent them! This year both of them celebrated their seventieth birthdays with great enthusiasm and thanksgiving. Ken said, 'How good the Lord is. He has given me my allotted time—three score years and ten—and now is giving me a bonus!' His wife Jean echoed those same words. The love and wisdom they have brought and share is a continual strengthening of all our lives, and we have grown as a church in love and understanding through them. They have a wonderful ministry and a zest for life which is contagious. When I look at them both I do not see two seventy-year-olds, I see two very special servants of the Lord exercising a powerful witness both within and outside the church, radiating his love which draws others to faith and to service. But should I be surprised as I read the Bible and see the people God used mightily? Many of them were well past retiring age, past old age, and yet they were the ones God chose to lead his people, to set out on new adventures, and to give vision, strength and hope to others.

'Grow old along with me, the best is yet to be' is often quoted by those who perhaps are seeing that the end of the road is in sight. But the phrase sparkles with richer meaning when the whole passage is read, for it goes on, 'The last of life, for which the first was made: Our times are in His hand who saith "A whole I planned, youth shows but half; trust God: see all nor be afraid!"' (Robert Browning, 1812–1889).

Paul, writing to the Corinthians, puts it all in perspective as he looks towards the glory of eternity: 'So we do not lose heart. Even though our outer nature is wasting away, our inner nature is being renewed day by day. For this slight momentary affliction is preparing us for an eternal weight of glory beyond all measure' (2 Corinthians 4:16 17). So what are a few grey hairs and the wrinkles and ravages of the years here, compared to such a glorious prospect? Eternal youth? No, something far, far better—eternal life!

Father, thank you for the moments, days and years you have given me. Thank you for rich gifts, the treasures of time and experience, lessons learned, sins forgiven, encouragements received. Thank you for companions along the way, the love of family and old and trusted friends, relationships born out of many years. Thank you for new friends who bring enthusiasm, zest and fun into life, for children who enable me to be a child again, to play, to discover, to wonder.

Thank you for the promise of tomorrow, and the assurance that whatever it brings, you are there already to welcome me and hold me safe, for all time and for eternity, world without end. Amen.

CHAPTER 30

Life is a battle

ROMANS 8:35 & 37

Who will separate us from the love of Christ? Will hardship, or distress, or persecution, or famine, or nakedness, or peril or sword? ... No, in all these things we are more than conquerors through him who loved us.

These are not the words of a leader, urging on his faltering troops, trying to inspire confidence even though they know the odds are stacked against them. These are the words of someone who has gone through all these things, and more, and knows the reality of the victory. From the moment of his conversion on the Damascus road, Saul, who became Paul, was in deep trouble. All the power and prestige he had on his side when he was a fanatical persecutor of the followers of Jesus had gone. He was regarded as a traitor, a fool, a dangerous turncoat, and as such had to be got rid of, before he could cause any more trouble. Whereas before Saul could rely on protection against any possible opposition, now he was on the run, aided only by a few of the followers of Jesus, who trusted that his conversion was real and not a trick. The once powerful, authoritative figure of Saul had to be led by the hand like a child to safety, unable to help himself, blinded and bowled over by that experience on the Damascus road. The conversion was real and lasting, and with his eyes opened, physically and spiritually, he devoted himself to sharing the good news of Jesus Christ, his one aim now to make Jesus known whatever it cost him. 'For I am not ashamed of the gospel; it is the power of God for salvation to everyone who has faith...' (Romans 1:16).

His life was completely changed and for his remaining years he would be continually travelling, enduring every kind of hardship. He describes some of them in his second letter to the Corinthians: 'Five times I have received from the Jews the forty lashes minus one. Three times I was beaten with rods. Once I received a stoning. Three times I was shipwrecked; for a night and a day I was adrift at sea; on frequent journeys, in danger from rivers, danger from bandits, danger from my own people, danger from Gentiles, danger in the city, danger in the wilderness, danger at sea, danger from false brothers and sisters, in toil and hardship, through many a sleepless night, hungry and thirsty, often without food, cold and naked. And besides other things I am under daily pressure because of my anxiety for all the churches' (2 Corinthians 11:24–28). And there was far more that could have been added. What a life! He endured physical, mental and spiritual hardships more than we can begin to imagine. He had trouble not only from outsiders but from Christians who caused so much turmoil amongst themselves and for their leaders that Paul almost despaired of them, and told them so in no uncertain terms.

Visiting, writing, building up groups, sorting out problems, he did all this in such adverse circumstances, also having to cope with his own illnesses and irksome restrictions. Then he was imprisoned, chained up, and finally executed. Why had he not settled for the quiet life, kept his head down, or found some distant place where he could live as a Christian without the hassle? I would not have been brave enough to ask him that question, for I can imagine him bearing down, eyes flashing, a voice like thunder saying to me, as he did to the Corinthians: 'Woe to me if I do not proclaim the gospel! ... I have become all things to all people that I might by all means save some!' (1 Corinthians 9:16 and 22). He had a passion for Christ, and a passion for people.

Passion is a strong word. We shy away from it, and maybe we would not like to be described as passionate about our faith because it sounds too much, over the top, unbalanced. Not the way to win friends or influence people. Yet we are passionate about so many things. Maybe our home or job, our family, sport, a hobby, an interest—we go for it one hundred per cent, single-minded, devoted, and yes, passionate. A young swimmer I met recently has given up everything to train, spending all her spare time at the swimming pool and with her coach. Swimming at 5.30am, training day in day out, forgoing all the things teenage girls usually find so exciting, and which she admits she does too. 'But I can't have that if I want to get to the top,' she told me. She has her eyes set on a future Olympic Games, and nothing else matters. Is it worth it? She thinks it is, and I hope it works out for her.

Read the history of the Christian Church—Paul was not the only one who endured such hardships. Delve into the records of missionary societies, the lives of those who gave up everything to share the good news of Jesus with people across the world, and paid the price with their lives. You do not need to go across the years or world either. Right here there are those experiencing hardship and peril in inner-city ministry—churches and premises vandalized, homes broken into, families bullied and harassed. Christian workers have been physically abused, threatened and attacked, and tragically a number have lost their lives. All the locks and alarm systems, the training in self-defence, will not eradicate the dangers, yet still men and women give up everything to go and serve joyfully, out of love and commitment to Jesus Christ. They know that in spite of the difficulties, nothing can separate them from the love of Christ. He is there with them, and it is not a matter of just 'getting through' but of being 'more than conquerors'—not just winning, but winning well.

Such people, in all parts of the world, in every stratum of society, demonstrate in their lives the victory by God's grace and the power of his Spirit. Famous household names are listed amongst them, giants of faith and action, but most are ordinary, quiet, unassuming people who get on with living for Jesus just where they are, coping with the snide remarks, the hurts and insults, the misunderstanding and ridicule. Some endure the most appalling personal situations, illness, handicaps, which would pull most of us under, and yet they show a strength, a power and a joy which draw others to discover for themselves the source of this extraordinary courage and persistence. I spoke to someone recently who was going through a very rough time with her next-door neighbours because she had dared to challenge them about their blatant bad behaviour towards an elderly neighbour living on the other side. I commented, 'I don't know how you put up with it all.' She patted my hand and said, 'Eh, don't you worry about me, Margaret, the Lord looks after me. Even when I get pushed in the muck he brings me up smelling of roses!' I looked at her and thought, 'And she's right!'

But what about those who do seem to go under, get stuck in the muck, are defeated, lose heart? What about the minister who is found hanging, having taken his own life in despair, feeling a failure? What about the young man who comes to faith in prison, is such a shining witness, and within three weeks of release is back inside again? What about the couple who have given up everything here in England to work in a hospital in Africa and are killed in an accident on the way to the airport? What about that brilliant Christian lawyer, giving himself tirelessly to helping the cause of political prisoners, suffering a massive stroke, unable to speak or move? What about... I could go on and on. We cannot avoid the disasters, failures, the questions that will not go away.

Paul was a realist: he knew all about failure too, in fact he struggled constantly with his own failures as well as those of the churches. He had seen Christians go under through persecution, torture, imprisonment—he had been party to it before his conversion. He had come to the conclusion that Jesus was a total failure, and rightly cut off in his prime before he could do any more damage, but Jesus had proved him wrong! Jesus had won the victory over death itself, and he had won the victory in Paul's life too, and that victory was complete—it was just the mopping-up battles that took the time. On the cross Jesus won the victory by love, the love that never ends, whatever happens—the eternal love of God.

Nothing, not even death itself, can ever separate us from the love of God, in Christ Jesus our Lord. That Paul knows, affirms, shares with us. 'We are more than conquerors through him who loved us.'

I hold to those words as I am confronted with success and failure, good and evil, life and death. But more than that, I know that Jesus holds to me, we are inseparable! And that is victory!

In John Bunyan's book *The Pilgrim's Progress* (1678) we read the moving words of Mr Valiant-for-Truth as he comes to the end of his pilgrimage of faith, through all the battles and difficulties:

> *I am going to my fathers, and though with great difficulty I am got hither, yet now I do not repent me of all the trouble I have been at to arrive where I am. My sword I give to him that shall succeed me in my pilgrimage, and my courage and skill to him that can get it. My marks and scars I carry with me, to be a witness for me that I have fought his battles who now will be my rewarder.*

Battle-scarred we may be, victorious we will be, that is for certain!

> *May I run the race before me,*
> *strong and brave to face the foe,*

looking only unto Jesus,
as I onward go.

May his beauty rest upon me,
as I seek the lost to win,
and may they forget the channel,
seeing only him.

Katie Barclay Wilkinson, 1859–1928

CHAPTER 31

Remember where you came from!

DEUTERONOMY 8:2

*Remember the long way that the Lord your God has led you these
forty years in the wilderness, in order to humble you, testing you
to know what was in your heart, whether or not you would keep
his commandments.*

When I get breathless with excitement, having a story to tell, I
remember myself as a child, dashing home, falling over myself and
my words in my eagerness to share what I had discovered, and my
mother saying, 'All right, calm down, begin at the beginning...' I
try to remind myself of her words when I rush along, describing
some event or experience without filling in the background of the
story. 'Go back to the beginning' is wise advice! It was back to the
beginning for the people to whom Moses was speaking in the
eighth chapter of Deuteronomy. He was reminding the Israelites of
God's commandments, his rules for life, as they prepared to enter
the promised land. Their eyes were fixed on the good times ahead,
the fulfilment of the promises of God, having a land of their own
instead of endless wandering around after their escape from slavery
in Egypt. They were full of what they were going to do and in
danger of forgetting the lessons of the past, the failures and the
successes, the bad times as well as the good, the times of rebellion
as well as of obedience. Their story, their history, was God's story,
'his-story', and it needed to be engraved on their hearts and memories so that they could go into the future with confidence and in
obedience. They were to remember where they had come from:
brought out of slavery, delivered by God, taught by God, tested by
God so as to become a strong people, a unity, to fulfil God's purposes for them.

And it is important for us to be aware of our history as a nation,
as a community, as families and individuals, for it helps us make
sense of the present and to anticipate the future. I constantly meet
people, especially from Australia, New Zealand and America, who

have come to this country 'to trace our ancestors'. They want to discover their roots, find the evidence through records, registers, tombstones, place names, that their forebears existed, were real people, and to discover the sort of lives they lived. Meeting Barbara recently, a delightful American, she told me of the thrill of visiting the actual place where her great-grandfather had lived and worked in Leeds. She said to me, 'I stood there and thought about him, and wondered how he had felt all those years ago when he made his decision to leave Leeds and set out for a new life in America.' He had gone out to America, worked in the woollen-mills there, set up his own company, which grew and prospered and continued to do so through the following generations. But he never forgot his roots, his humble beginnings, which had provided him with the knowledge and the spur to be a success in a new land. Now his great-granddaughter could stand where he had stood many years before and feel a oneness, a sense of belonging, and of thanksgiving for him and what he had passed on to her down the years and generations. Now she would be able to pass on that knowledge in the writing up of the family tree for new generations—the record of where they had come from, starting at the beginning, going through to them and into the future.

I meet people who reflect the other side of the search for roots, who have been unable to trace family, some who had been adopted many years before, and have no record of their background, their blood relatives. One, who had tried every possible line of enquiry and agency without success, said to me sadly, 'I feel in limbo, that I do not belong anywhere, I don't know who I am.' She was happily married, with a lovely family, but had this enormous gap in her life because she had no background, no history, nothing to help her make sense of who she was and what she was.

In the Bible we have the story from the beginning of God's family, the old covenant, and the new, to which we all belong. We have our roots in God. Yes, we all have our own history, the reminders of where we came from, but more than this, we know *who* we came from, the source of our life. Our problem is that we soon forget, *choosing* to forget in our eagerness to do our own thing, go our own way, and then we wonder why we get ourselves into difficulties! 'Remember all the way that the Lord God has led you...' is for us today, as well as for those wandering ex-slaves heading for God's promised land. But what were they charged to remember? That God, the Lord their God, had a loving purpose for them, but that to achieve his purpose they needed to be taught, disciplined, loved, supported along the way.

God could have lifted them out of slavery in Egypt in one almighty act, and put them straight into a rich, fertile land, given them power and strength, made them a mighty people. Instead there were forty years of trudging through difficult and dangerous territory, knowing failure and frustration, even to the point of mutiny, turning their backs on their leaders and even on God. There must have been an easier way, so why didn't God take them the short pretty route rather than on this long arduous trail? He did it out of love for them, so that they might grow up, learn the lessons of faith and obedience, of knowing he was their God, their Father. Yes, learning by their own mistakes, learning the hard way that God's way, God's commandments, God's laws were for their well-being, to equip them to live, to prosper, to be his people. They would prosper, they would inherit the promised land, they would praise God, and be successful and safe, full materially, physically and spiritually. 'You shall eat your fill and bless the Lord your God for the good land he has given you' (Deuteronomy 8:10) was the promise and the experience, but always with the reminder that they should not be so taken up with what they enjoyed that they did not remember the lessons of the past. It was a message that was given, forgotten, taken up again, over and over, and it now comes to us. 'You shall remember the long way that the Lord your God has led you...'

A year to the day after I slid unceremoniously down an Italian hillside, badly breaking my foot and ankle, and having to face several months of restrictions, pain, discomfort and frustration, I stood looking out over another hillside across to Simons Seat in the Yorkshire Dales, with Bolton Abbey Moor on the horizon. I had driven over from our home in Selby to Parcevall Hall, the Bradford diocesan retreat house where I was to conduct a quiet day for clergy wives from the Bradford diocese. On a lovely summer's evening I had explored the gardens, clambered up the path to the terrace, and now stood looking out on a landscape of awe-inspiring beauty. Here I was, a year on from that accident, the date reminding me not just of my fall, but of all I had learned and experienced through the past year—not all of it easy or pleasant. It had been hard to be totally at the mercy of others, even to the point of having to ask to be taken to the toilet—a new experience! To be unable to go where I wanted, do what I wanted, be what I wanted. To be pushed around for a while in a wheelchair, and one bearing the inscription 'On loan from Help the Aged'. Very good for my growth in humility and understanding! To be frightened to death being pushed across a busy road, seeing traffic bearing down at me, and wondering whether it would avoid me. Then learning to walk on crutches, and being treated as though I was a child, and a rather thick one at that! Learning that I was not quite as tough as I thought, nor as kind and good either! I learned how much I was loved and cared for, and how forgiving people and God were, and how they understood me far more than I had realized when I rushed along doing my 'I'm in charge' act. I had learned what it was like to be weak and helpless, to fail miserably not just at negotiating Italian paths but in my relationships with others—in learning to hold my tongue, to think before I spoke, and to appreciate just what others had to put up with in me. The memories of a year came flooding back as I stood looking out at the scene before me, and thinking of the prospects of the day ahead, with so much joy and anticipation. Would I want that year over again? Many parts of it no, and yet it had been a time when I had learned so much more about life, myself, other people and God. It had been a package deal, so I praised God for it as I stood enjoying the present, which was a foretaste of the promised land.

Just one year—but I look back over many, many years, and I remember, and I reflect, and I thank God for the years, and pray I will never forget them, and what has happened in them. Yes, as my mother had told me, 'All right, calm down, begin at the beginning...' Begin at the beginning, remember the years, the experiences, good and bad. Remember the things you took for granted, the little things which were so important for sustaining life, ensuring growth and development. Remember the experiences which strengthened faith and resolve. Remember the failures which made you realize your own weakness and need for help, and also helped you sympathize with others, understand them, and be able to point them to the source of forgiveness and strength, and be thankful for it all.

Dr Edward Norman, writing in his Meditation column in *The Daily Telegraph*, recently wrote this, 'The trouble is that people today are not enormously given to expressions of gratitude. Our culture, indeed, encourages a sense of entitlements and benefits rather than thankfulness for what we have already received.' He went on to express the hope that 'we may return to the kind of awe which once promoted obedience to the will of God'. I echo his words as I look back with both thankfulness and a sense of awe over the years, over the last year, over this very day. Now to the future! The promises of God are true, I know that from experience. What awaits me on the next stage of my journey he knows, he has already taken care of. What he asks me to do is remember the past, live for him today, and trust him for tomorrow.

Day by day, we magnify thee,
and we worship thy name, ever world without end.
Vouchsafe, O Lord to keep us this day without sin.
O Lord have mercy upon us, have mercy upon us.
O Lord, let thy mercy lighten upon us, as our trust is in thee.
O Lord in thee have I trusted, let me never be confounded.'

Te Deum Laudamus from *The Book of Common Prayer*

CHAPTER 32

Journey's end

REVELATION 21:1–7

*Then I saw a new heaven and a new earth; for the first
heaven and the first earth had passed away, and the sea was no
more. And I saw the holy city, the new Jerusalem, coming
down out of heaven from God, prepared as a bride adorned for
her husband. And I heard a loud voice from the throne
saying, 'See, the home of God is among mortals. He will dwell
with them as their God; they will be his peoples, and God
himself will be with them; he will wipe every tear from their eyes.
Death will be no more; mourning and crying and pain will
be no more, for the first things have passed away.' And the one
who was seated on the throne said, 'See, I am making all
things new.' Also he said, 'Write this, for these words
are trustworthy and true.' Then he said to me, 'It is done! I am
the Alpha and the Omega, the beginning and the end.
To the thirsty I will give water as a gift from the spring of
the water of life. Those who conquer will inherit these things,
and I will be their God and they will be my children.'*

The forecasters had promised rain, and the sullen early morning
clouds had seemed to confirm it, but by noon the sun had broken
through, dispersing the clouds, giving a clear blue sky, a perfect
spring day. It was the day of Alf's funeral, taking place only eleven
weeks after his wife Nancy's. We could not be sad for Alf, but we
felt the sadness of the family experiencing the pain of bereavement
twice in such a short time.

Adrian, a member of our church who is training for the ministry,
was home for the Easter break and had assisted me with the funeral service. We now stood together in the cemetery after saying
goodbye to Alf's family and friends who had come on from church
to share in the committal. We watched the cars wending their way
out of the gates, and then began to make our way to where our car
was parked. Adrian remarked that it was the first time he had been
in Selby cemetery and so I began pointing out the headstones of
those whose funerals I had taken over the years, so many of them

dear friends, members of St James'. Many of them Adrian had never met, as they had gone before he and his wife Alison had arrived in Selby, so I explained who they were, and something about their lives, the special things I remembered about them, what they had meant to me. As we walked together in the sunshine I thought too of another churchyard, over in the village of Gawsworth, the home of my parents. The ancient church there is set amid the beauty of the Cheshire countryside with the hills in the distance, and across from the church like two sentinels, the black and white Old Rectory, and Gawsworth Hall, with the picturesque pools in front. It is a popular beauty spot, and people come from many miles, indeed many parts of the world, to visit the village and surroundings.

My mother enjoyed a walk round the village whenever I went home, and the churchyard was always a must. When our children were small they came with us to feed the ducks in the pools, to chase excitedly round the edges, but when we got into the churchyard they became quiet, and attentive to their granny as she told them stories of people she had known who were buried there. They loved to take some flowers to put on the grave of a former rector of Gawsworth, and although they had never known him they always wanted to hear about him and make sure he had some flowers. I think he would have enjoyed their visits! Towards the end of her life my mother still enjoyed walking down to the churchyard with me, and I remember her one day standing there, with a faraway look in her eyes, saying very firmly, 'I must be getting old, I have more friends in here than in the village now.' She had outlived many of her friends, but she did not make her comment with any sadness or regret, it was just a fact of life. She had happy memories, and her friends were at rest, and she knew it would not be so long before she would be too.

Walking with Adrian in Selby, introducing him to my old friends, reminded me of my mother's words, and of her attitude to death. She did not fear it, she accepted it, and in fact welcomed it. Just before she died she spoke about going to heaven, and I remarked, 'Well, you will know plenty of people there, Mum. There's so-and-so, and so-and-so...' She had looked at me with the expression she used when I was a child and I hadn't quite got her point, and said, 'There are no strangers in heaven!' Point taken! In every funeral I take I think of those words, and each time I say the words, 'We have entrusted ... to God's merciful keeping, in sure and certain hope of the resurrection to eternal life through our Lord Jesus Christ,' I ask myself, 'Margaret, do you believe that? Is it really true, or is this the end?' It is a hard moment or two, a challenge, but thank God I have always been able to say—and mean, and know—'Praise God, I believe it. I know it is true.'

Death is no respecter of persons. It comes to everyone, and yet when it happens it is always a shock, a surprise, 'unexpected'. There is something in us which makes us reluctant to accept that death comes to our loved ones, our friends, and to us. It is not something that just happens to other people. We are all mortal. Of course, when it happens to a child, or someone in the prime of life, through a tragic accident or from a cruel disease, we feel they have been cheated out of life, they had not had their entitlement of years, of time. These days even the biblical 'three score years and ten' seems quite young, especially to those who are nearing it, or have passed it. We are, as a society in this country, living longer, and as I look around the community I live in, and those within our church, they all seem to be very active even into their eighties and nineties. In fact only a few days ago I had the pleasure of taking a lady of one hundred and three around York Minster. She was in a wheelchair, but very alert and interested in everything, sharing with us her memories of the time when she was an active and regular member of the congregation. After I had said a prayer with her and before she left, she grasped my hand and said, 'And now I want to pray for you, and everyone else in this wonderful place.' Her voice was steady and clear, her face radiant, and I felt so blessed by her. One hundred and three, and still going strong, but we all have to admit that age catches up on us—'the sands of time' eventually run out, and what then? Why do we so desperately cling to this life, I wonder? Because we all do. It is only when we realize that this life is but part of eternity, and prepare ourselves for the future, that we can approach whatever comes with serenity and hope. Bishop Michael Marshall said recently in an article, 'What we like to call life is at best only a cut-flower existence, doomed to fading and the loss of bloom.' And the novelist Victor Hugo (1802–1885) wrote, 'When I go down to the grave, I can say like so many others that I have finished my day's work; but I cannot say I have finished my life. Another day's work will begin in the morning. The tomb is not a blind alley, it is a thoroughfare.'

Heaven will not be a continuation of this phase with all its restrictions, but the entrance into a new dimension of life. We will still be 'us' but the 'us' God intended, in a perfect relationship with him and with all the other inhabitants of his eternal kingdom.

Over and over again people say to me, 'If only I could have a new start... have my life over again, it would be so different...' The fact is that we cannot turn the clock back, biological or any other, even with the latest creams, diets, and treatments. At best we can only cover up the inevitable! What God offers is 'all things new' and I know of no better offer!

The words from Revelation 21 are very special to me. I use them so often at funeral services, and always with assurance and joy, because I can share the comfort of God's word with those who are mourning, crying, in pain, and his word says that those who will trust in his promises will inherit the kingdom. They are a reminder too of the words of Jesus to his friends, 'Do not be afraid, little flock, for it is your Father's good pleasure to give you the kingdom' (Luke 12:32). They are words I often read to myself, and find I am always excited by them, I look forward to being part of that kingdom one day, enjoying all that God has prepared in his love for his children. I can look forward to being there not because of what I have done, but because of what Jesus Christ has done for me. He has indeed 'opened the kingdom of heaven to all believers', to those who trust him, having faith even as tiny and seemingly insignificant as a grain of seed.

Yet the question is put to me over and over again: 'But what about those who did not believe, those who turned their back on God, those who never showed any interest? What about those whom I love but who do not share my faith? Will we ever meet again?' I can only say that in scripture the promise is clear that those who trust in Christ have already entered into eternal life. It is here and now and for always, so we can know for ourselves, that is definite. As for others—who are we to judge what goes on between them and God even at the last moment of life? Who are we to pretend to understand their hearts, what has affected or damaged them, what has stopped them from believing? Who knows the human heart but God? Do we not trust him to do what is right, what is loving, what is merciful, what is just? I think of God's answer to Job's questionings: 'Where were you when I laid the foundation of the earth? Tell me, if you have understanding' (Job 38:4). In other words, 'I am the creator, this is my world, I will do what I will do.' How dare we question him, ask him to account for his dealings? But we do.

For me the picture that comes to mind is the time when Jesus recalled Peter to his service. Peter had deserted his Lord, sworn he had never even heard of him, let alone been a friend or companion. But on the seashore Jesus gave Peter a second chance, recommissioned him, said again those words of invitation: 'Follow me.' What amazing love to do that, to trust him, want him, invite him! But Jesus did. Then Peter, as he sets off, turns round and sees someone else, John, in the background. 'Lord, what about him?' Peter wants to know, and the reply comes, '...what is that to you? Follow me!' (John 21:19–22). I think about the future, looking forward to what is in store, which I know will be greater than I could ever begin to imagine or hope. I delight in the promise of God to make all things new—and that includes me. *I* will be new, I will be the Margaret he intended, planned for in love, and gave his Son for. And as I am taken up with excitement, with longing, with the desire to make sure everybody knows about it, I, like Peter, often say, 'But what about...?' and the loving but firm reply I get is the one Peter got: 'What is that to you? Follow me!'

The invitation comes to us all: 'Follow me.' Sometimes we need reminding of our calling. Often we have to be picked up, brought back, set on the way again. There are times when we get diverted, when we wilfully choose to go off in a completely different direction! There are moments when we despair and say, 'I can't go on,' or equally, 'I'll do it my way, I can do it myself, thank you.' Yet along with the others, some known to us, many strangers (until we get to heaven of course!) but all part of the family, we travel on, called and enabled to follow by his grace. And along the way there is always provided 'something for the journey'—that special something that makes the journey not only possible but an adventure of faith, hope and love, with that sure and certain hope that soon we will ourselves see that new heaven and new earth. We will see the one seated on the throne, and be part of the glory of eternity.

All things new! Does he mean us? He most certainly does!

From earth's wide bounds, from ocean's farthest coast,
through gates of pearl streams in the countless host.
Singing to Father, Son and Holy Ghost,
Alleluia! Alleluia!

William Walsham How, 1823–1897

CHAPTER 33

Thank you for everything

Bless the Lord, O my soul,
and all that is within me,
bless his holy name.
Bless the Lord, O my soul,
and do not forget all his benefits.

Sitting in the Abbey that night, listening to the choir singing the anthem 'Litany to the Holy Spirit', my mind went back over the last twenty-five years—to the day. For it was in Selby Abbey on 31 May 1973 that I had been licensed as Parish Worker to serve as non-stipendiary minister in my own parish of St James, Selby—the 'church around the corner' from the Abbey. I assumed it would be a temporary measure until a new vicar was appointed, that I was filling in for a while. But during the actual licensing, as I knelt before the Bishop of Selby and he prayed, 'May the Lord give you wisdom, courage and strength and love to do his will' as he laid his hands upon me, I knew with blinding certainty that I was not entering into a temporary arrangement, for the convenience of a specific situation, but I was embarking on a lifetime commitment. What that was to mean I hadn't a clue, but it was sealed between God and me that night. He would provide all that would be need-ed, the wisdom, courage, strength and love that the Bishop had prayed for me. All I had to do was trust and obey!

Twenty-five years ago, a long time. What had happened during those twenty-five years? The Church of England had gone through unimaginably great changes, and I had been very much part of that change, being made deaconess four years after my licensing, deacon ten years later, and after seven more, ordained priest. Twenty-one years from the realization that God had called me to the ministry, to priesthood, and the varying experiences along the way. Twenty-one years—certainly a wonderful coming of age! But now, four more years on, I celebrated twenty-five years in the same parish, and that morning there had been a wonderful celebration of those twenty-five years. New banners in glorious colours had appeared, sparkling, winking, almost dancing as they hung from the pillars. There was a large iced cake in the shape of a Bible, flowers, cards, and the presentation of two reclining chairs for the garden so that Peter and I could spend some time relaxing together in the sunshine. All around us were beaming faces, the buzz of excitement, songs of praise raising the roof as together we thanked God for his goodness to us as a church family, past and present.

Peter and I looked out at a sea of faces, and knew afresh what being part of the family of God was all about. In 1973 the day had been Ascension Day, in 1998 it fell on the day of Pentecost—the perfect day for a celebration. I thought back to the time when I had heard the words, 'Be filled with the Spirit', of my fear, puzzlement, and finally the leap of faith when I said, 'I don't know what this is all about, but the answer is "yes"!' and knew in that moment of opening myself to whatever God wanted to do in my life a freedom, an acceptance and a joy, that could sustain me in whatever happened, wherever he put me. Of the way then opening up into the ministry, and... well, the rest all followed. One of my favourite expressions is, 'God opens doors and I fall through them' because it explains so much that seemed beyond possibility. As door after door opened up, I went on falling through them, sometimes painfully, mostly joyfully, usually unexpectedly, but always coming through the other side. I never cease to be amazed at what God can do, especially with such raw material. Anything is possible with him, for I see it happening over and over again, and not just in my own life but in the lives of so many who are also prepared to fall through his open doors.

Had I been told on 31 May 1973 that twenty-five years later I would still be serving in that same church, I would have laughed. 'Twenty-five years? You must be joking! Who knows where I might be by then?' But it was no joke, just sheer joy! Psalm 103 has always been a favourite of mine, a hymn of gratitude to God for all his goodness, not only in this life, 'but the steadfast love of the Lord is from everlasting to everlasting' (v. 17). David knew that his God was not for this life only, but for eternity. He recognized his own frailty and need, that as a mere man he had a brief stay here on this earth, and the picture he gives of the wind blowing over the fields sums up that short span of life. Beautiful flowers or plain grass are transient, and so are we. That in itself could be a frightening thought, for what use is life if it is gone in a moment? David looks above and beyond this life to the God who sustains us here on earth yet has his throne in heaven. He rules over all, and will reign for ever and ever.

David was the young shepherd boy who became the great king. Warrior, leader, poet, musician, chosen by God to lead his people, but still mortal, still vulnerable. He who was so in tune with God sank to the depths of sin, committing murder and adultery. In this psalm he points us to eternity, but also reminds us of our earthiness, weakness and failure, and of the God who knows and understands, who has compassion, and forgives. David speaks for himself, and he also speaks for us. It begins as his solo, then he draws us in as a chorus, calling even the angels to join in, with the orchestra of all creation, before returning to the beginning—'Bless the Lord O my soul'—speaking again to himself out of his own condition and experience of the mighty, loving Lord God.

The psalm has a completeness, covering all of life's experiences, so comprehensive in its view of human nature, but also seeing men and women as created by God with an eternal future. It speaks of forgiveness and healing, which surely go together, for however physically fit or mentally able we may be, we fail miserably in our relationships over and over again. Think of the way we treat our fellow human beings—often those nearest and dearest to us—our failure to respond to the needs of others, our lack of concern for the plight of those who are suffering, our arrogance in thinking we can pull ourselves up by our own boot straps, our disregard of God's commands and also of his love. Would you call these things 'iniquity'? It is a strong word, containing every evil thought and deed imaginable, but basically meaning 'unrighteousness'—thinking, saying, doing anything that is not right. I find that a warning to me as I feebly try to argue my case for not being included in the grouping of those who commit iniquity. I know I have not a leg to stand on, and I am likely to fall flat on my face unless I avail myself of the forgiveness and support God holds out to me.

Unacknowledged, unconfessed sin results in our being diseased, not at ease with ourselves, our fellows or God, and can give rise to physical as well as emotional and spiritual problems. God offers us release and relief and in fact far more than that, for he lifts us out of the pit we have dug for ourselves, or which others have pushed us into, and gives us a new life. He doesn't just pull us up and leave us, but crowns us with his love and mercy. It is a picture of the highest honour possible: a crown on our heads! And his love and mercy are more glorious and lasting than the most bejewelled crown of precious gold. I'll go for love and mercy any time and all the time. What price earthly glory and honour in the light of what God offers us?

The more I read this psalm, think about it, apply it to myself, the more I feel compelled to share with others the good news it contains. It is too good to keep to myself, and this is surely how David felt as he sang this great hymn of thanksgiving and praise. And it has come down through the centuries to touch our lives, to draw us into new experiences of God's goodness and love.

Looking back at my life, and particularly over the last twenty-five years, this psalm has captured again for me what it has all been about. But I am not just looking back at times past, but thinking of a present joyful reality. It speaks of the here and now, today, the present tense.

One of the best-known and best-loved hymns of praise is the one by Henry Francis Lyte, which he based on Psalm 103. Written over one hundred and fifty years ago, it still expresses the joy that David knew, and which has been proclaimed and shared by men and women of every age and condition.

> *Praise my soul, the king of heaven,*
> *To his feet thy tribute bring,*
> *Ransomed, healed, restored, forgiven,*
> *Who like thee his praise should sing?*
> *Alleluia! Alleluia!*
> *Praise the everlasting King.*

He reminds us that 'Father like, he tends and spares us, Well our feeble frame he knows...' and then, like David, he calls out to the angels in heaven, to all creation to join in the song:

> *Angels, help us to adore him,*
> *Ye behold him face to face,*
> *Sun and moon bow down before him,*
> *Dwellers all in time and space.*
> *Alleluia! Alleluia!*
> *Praise with us the God of grace.*

Father, For all that is past, I thank and praise you. For today, I praise and thank you. For all that is to come, in time and eternity, I thank and praise you. For steadfast love and mercy which you have shown me in the past, still show today and will continue to show me in the future, I thank and praise you.

Bless the Lord O my soul, and all that is within me, bless his holy name!